Heading to the

Holy Land

ANDRE MOUBARAK

How to Prepare, Plan, and Pray
for a Life-Changing Journey

To every Tour Leader that crossed my path
To every Spirit-filled Divine moment we shared together
Your passion, love and servant hearts
I deeply admire...

I dedicate this book to you all
Thank You!

Table of Contents

Foreword

My first trip to Israel was totally orchestrated by other Tour Leaders and motivated by the desire to share a fun vacation with my daughter. As we traveled through the land where God chose to unfold His redemptive story, I was convinced that I would be coming back often and bringing others so that they could experience the same faith-changing journey in the Holy Land.

Within days of arriving home, I had a group of friends lined up and excited about traveling to Israel, but it was quickly apparent that my zeal far outstripped my capability to arrange a great experience and itinerary for them. Andre and Marie came to the rescue by expertly answering my questions and crafting a custom itinerary. Now Andre is making his trip-planning expertise available to all trip leaders in his latest book, "Heading to the Holy Land".

Andre is intimately familiar with the culture and context that shapes the land of Israel and is a master at captivating tour groups with the Biblical significance of each site along the way. By sharing his experience, gleaned from guiding countless groups, "Heading to the Holy Land" equips trip leaders to transform what otherwise would be a fun vacation into a life-changing journey that stretches travelers' faith, expands their understanding of Scripture and the land where it all unfolded.

I encourage every trip leader to start their journey in the pages of "Heading to the Holy Land" to save time and money, and most importantly, to create a life-changing journey for travelers.

Tour Leader Anne-Marie Von Kahle

From the Author

I want to share with you how this book came into reality. I have been a tour guide for more than twenty years. Those twenty years, like twenty days, passed in a blink of an eye, I did not feel the time. Our lives are significant in this world, and every minute of our life is valuable, especially as a teacher of scripture. I always say, "Time waits for nobody, and nobody waits for time."

Ever since the very first group I ever guided and before gaining all this experience, many Tour Leaders encouraged me to gather all this information and knowledge into a book. Finally, I did it! Two decades worth of material from Twins Tours & Travel were collected into this practical book – a professional reference for Tour Leaders, Pastors, and laymen. Basically, any person with a vision to bring a group to Israel, and yet has no idea where to start and what to do, this book is for you – *Heading to the Holy Land.*

Heading to the Holy Land is a simple read that explains from A to Z all the steps on how to prepare a group visiting Israel. This book will equip you with the right information on how to understand all the legal, ethical, and even cultural considerations. All this is designed to help you become a GREAT and equipped Tour Leader, managing your group both in Israel and the West Bank.

One last thing, part of my vision for this book is to bring more kingdom transformation to the many groups that visit Israel. I long in my heart for God's people to see the Land of the Bible – Israel is full of spiritual treasure that is buried in the heart of this world in the Middle East. When you visit the land, this treasure will be yours, and the Word of God will come alive in a way you haven't experienced before.

I pray that this book will inspire every Tour Leader, every Minister, every church member, or you as an individual pilgrim to come to this land of the Bible and meet with us.

Andre Moubarak

Welcome to Twins Tours & Travel Ltd

Twins Tours & Travel LTD is a local Christian Arab agency specializing in building customized tour packages to the Holy Land, the birthplace of Judaism and Christianity. Our privilege as local Christians is having the opportunity to travel, not only in Israel – but throughout the entire West Bank with no restrictions whatsoever, and we look forward to sharing that experience with you. Experience the Bible's living history first-hand as you retrace the path of the Patriarchs and walk in the footsteps of Jesus. It is our aim that you and your fellow travelers will gain greater insight into the Scriptures as you connect with the land and the local Body of Christ. It has been both humbling and a privilege to see numerous lives transformed as our groups experience the God of the Scripture on a personal level through the intentional interaction with the Land of the Bible.

Mission Statement

To provide a journey of identity through learning the culture, the customs, and the context of Scripture through Jesus' Middle Eastern eyes, mind, and heart.

Our Experience

In our experience of more than 20 years, most people leave this land changed forever. For those who have never been to Israel, it is hard to describe how much of a difference it makes to come and stand in the land of the Bible and see it for yourself. We have often heard it described as suddenly seeing in color after living in a world of black and white. There is no doubt that coming to the Holy Land will inject new life into the faith walk of tour participants with Jesus of Nazareth, and unveil a new appreciation for His Word.

In addition to offering Biblical study tours, we also offer a variety of tours, each with a different focus:

- Biblical Study Tours
- Faith Pilgrimages
- Service/Volunteer/Ministry Projects
- Intercessory Prayer Journeys
- Personally Customized/Specialized/Themed or Concept Tours
- Conferences/Concerts

Vision Statement

We pursue unity between the Western and Eastern Churches by building bridges in personal interaction between the living stones to foster relationships of mutual blessing and understanding between them. Through personal experience, God gives revelation of His heart for every tongue, tribe, and nation which matures the Body of Christ in bringing reconciliation, unity, and a testimony that Jesus is Lord.

To achieve these goals, we invite groups to experience the Holy Land and its people in depth from an indigenous Evangelical Christian perspective. Come join us in bringing your prayers to life!

Detailed Vision Statement

We pursue a real unity which does not imply becoming homogenous or agreeing on everything. Real unity recognizes that no man (or culture) is an island. We each have strengths and weaknesses and we benefit from diversity when we achieve unity that produces mutual blessing.

Achieving unity requires a revelation from God on three levels:

1. Awareness – God reveals to us that there are Christians from a completely different culture and with a completely different history – Middle Eastern Christians.

    a. Awareness begins with realizing that there are Palestinians Christians which are not Muslim background believers (MBBs) but rather Christians from birth and often for many generations.

    b. Awareness continues with the revelation that Jesus didn't give His disciples the King James Bible with His words in red. Jesus spoke Hebrew and Aramaic. Middle Eastern Christians today speak the same Semitic languages of Aramaic, Hebrew and Arabic.

    c. Awareness, ultimately, includes revelation that Jerusalem is the birthplace of all Christianity and not the Western Nations which receive the most media attention. There is something holy and rooted about Eastern Christianity that Western Christianity only vaguely knows exists!

2. Understanding – God reveals the culture and history of these Middle Eastern Christians and gives us the ability to see how they see. Their perspective of the scripture becomes one in which we understand and can also access.

3. Appreciation – God reveals his heart for these Middle Eastern Christians and the beauty He sees in that culture and perspective. Co-founder Tony likes to say, "We still carry the smell of Christ." It may be different and because it is foreign, that smell may not appeal at first. But with understanding and connection, a level of unity can be achieved which produces appreciation for the Middle Eastern Christians and the "smell of Christ" still present in this culture.

    a. Appreciation begins with humility of seeing weaknesses in one's own culture/perspective that could be strengths in the other cultures/perspectives.

b. Appreciation also realizes that Eastern Christianity may look very different and have weaknesses, but the strengths Western Christianity has to offer must come from a place of service and not superiority.

c. Appreciation also includes a decision not to vilify any of the groups in the Middle East: Jews, or Palestinians. The saying is, "If you choose, you lose."

The Western and Eastern Churches which Twins Tours is trying to unify has many distinct differences. As mentioned previously, it is incumbent on all to be aware of these differences, understand these differences, and ultimately, appreciate these differences. Here are some of the noteworthy differences:

Western Christianity	**Eastern Christianity**
Romance Languages (English, Spanish, etc.)	Semitic Languages (Aramaic, Hebrew, Arabic)
Organizational	Relational
Individualistic	Communal
Rigid/Boxy	Fluid
Formal without many customs	Informal with many customs
Values Mind and Thought	Values Heart and Emotions
Theoretical	Action-oriented
Timely	Improvisational

These Christian communities also differ tremendously in their history. These historical differences impact the perspective of Christians from these communities even today. Western Christianity was integrated with national governments even ruling over large sections of Europe at times. This produced a more hierarchical oriented Christianity and one which naturally thinks institutionally. Eastern Christianity began with almost 400 years of persecution and attempted to survive under various ruling nations and people. This produced a community oriented relationally.

Both Western and Eastern churches have valuable natural strengths and Twins Tours would like to help each side to be aware, understand and ultimately appreciate those strengths. We recognize that our rich indigenous Christian heritage and culture utilizing the Aramaic and Hebrew sources of scripture can be an asset to Western Christians.

Twins Tours serves as a natural bridge because of its connection to Messianic Jews, Orthodox Jews, Arab Christians, Arab Muslims, and Western Christians. We want to help others build bridges in personal interaction in three main ways:

1. Bridging to Arab Christians
2. Bridging to Arab Muslims
3. Bridging to Jews

A bridge, by definition, is a two-way connection. A weak bridge cannot handle a heavy load. Similarly, a weak relational bridge cannot handle heavy topics and in order to bring true unity, we must be able to talk about the heavy concepts plaguing the Middle East. But we start building and recognize not all relational bridges are ready for the weight of some issues. We appreciate any and all bridges as they do represent an awareness, understanding, and appreciation of the "other" to an extent.

In the end, every relational bridge comes down to a personal connection. To this end, Twins Tours fosters personal connections between tourists and local communities. The type and depth of connection is dictated by the size of the group.

- **Ministry:** For groups of 10-25 people, these groups get hands on with locals often in their personal homes.

- **Interaction:** For groups of 26-50 people, these groups visit locals in their ministry environment.

- **Exposure:** For groups of 51+ people, these groups are visited by locals who share about their life, ministry, and experiences.

Three quick examples of these opportunities:

A Ministry Group can have one- or two-nights homestay with a Palestinian family in Bethlehem or West Bank. They will enjoy the food prepared by the host and learn the village culture in a way that brings the bible to life. They will hear the family stories and have fun learning from each other. In this way they will understand the daily challenges of the family, build trust, and begin a lifelong friendship.

Though many people want to do "ministry" in Israel and Palestine, we have found that pastors first need to build a relationship with the people before "doing ministry" in order to be effective.

An Interaction Group can have a Shabbat dinner with a Jewish family. They will learn about Shabbat and Jewish family values and the daily life in Israel. They will learn a Jewish perspective that will help the Bible come to life. The experience will probably stay with the group longer than the guide teachings at a given site.

An Exposure Group can have a Jewish Rabbi meet the group for a lecture about Jewish-Christian relations. Then that same group can meet a Palestinian Christian farmer and hear his story as well. Another option is to bring a Muslim-background believer (MBB) to share his testimony. These experiences expose the group to a world they may not have even been aware of previously.

For those who want to minister to locals, they must have a relationship with local pastors and appreciation for the good in the culture. It is important not to give solutions until a relationship is established. In the beginning of a relationship, it is important not to judge but just hear the hearts of the people who are hurt and need someone to listen to them.

In this way, a tourist can relate to the history and ancient lessons rooted in the Bible and also to the living stones. We read in 1 Peter 2:5, "You yourselves like living stones are being built up as a spiritual house, to be a holy priesthood, to offer spiritual sacrifices acceptable to God through Jesus Christ."

We are all the living stones which are being built up together. Sometimes tourists forget the local believers who are living stones far more precious than the ancient stones of the Western Wall or Caesarea. They are a holy priesthood with spiritual sacrifices and gifts to give. They are the continuation of 2,000 years of what Jesus started here in the Land. There is a continuation of biblical events with events going on TODAY in the land.

To bring the living stones into unity, the wounds of the past will need to be healed through reconciliation. Some of these wounds include the wealth of the Western church, neglect and even complete ignorance of the Eastern Church, a Western superiority complex, and indigeneity pride of the Eastern church.

Clearly, the vision for unity has not yet been achieved. It has grown but the vast majority of the Body of Christ is still far from unified. What will real unity look like when achieved? The mutual appreciation we've discussed, will result also in mutual blessing. There will be a cooperation between the different parts of the Body just like the eyes, hands, feet, and ears of our physical bodies work in harmony (1 Corinthians 12:15-25).

> "15 Now if the foot should say, "Because I am not a hand, I do not belong to the body," it would not for that reason stop being part of the body. 16 And if the ear should say, "Because I am not an eye, I do not belong to the body," it would not for that reason stop being part of the body. 17 If the whole body were an eye, where would the sense of hearing be? If the whole body were an ear, where would the sense of smell be? 18 But in fact God has placed the parts in the body, every one of them, just as he wanted them to be. 19 If they were all one part, where would the body be? 20 As it is, there are many parts, but one body.
>
> 21 The eye cannot say to the hand, "I don't need you!" And the head cannot say to the feet, "I don't need you!" 22 On the contrary, those parts of the body that seem to be weaker are indispensable, 23 and the parts that we think are less honorable we treat with special honor. And the parts that are unpresentable are treated with special modesty, 24 while our presentable parts need no special treatment. But God has put the body together, giving greater honor to the parts that lacked it, 25 so that there should be no division in the body, but that its parts should have equal concern for each other."

The strengths of one part of the Body of Christ assist in the weakness of another part. The Body functioning properly is a healthy whole and each part is blessed by being part of the whole.

In addition to mutual blessing, unity brings a testimony to unbelievers (John 17:20-23) and the power of the holy spirit (Acts 2:1-4).

20 "My prayer is not for them alone. I pray also for those who will believe in me through their message, 21 that all of them may be one, Father, just as you are in me and I am in you. May they also be in us so that the world may believe that you have sent me. 22 I have given them the glory that you gave me, that they may be one as we are one— 23 I in them and you in me—so that they may be brought to complete unity. Then the world will know that you sent me and have loved them even as you have loved me."

"When the day of Pentecost came, they were all together in one place. 2 Suddenly a sound like the blowing of a violent wind came from heaven and filled the whole house where they were sitting. 3 They saw what seemed to be tongues of fire that separated and came to rest on each of them. 4 All of them were filled with the Holy Spirit and began to speak in other tongues as the Spirit enabled them."

In a land divided by politics, language, and tribal loyalties, unity of believers which transcends politics, language and tribal loyalties is remarkable to the unbeliever. The love of Jesus is given a stage which all can appreciate. The heart of God is not just that as many to be saved as possible in a general sense. It's not a generic love to mankind, it's a personal love and appreciation for the beauty of diversity. In the age to come every tongue, tribe, and nation will come up to Jerusalem to worship *(Revelation 5:9)*.

" 9 And they sang a new song, saying:
"You are worthy to take the scroll
and to open its seals,
because you were slain,
and with your blood you purchased for God

persons from every tribe and language
and people and nation."

We serve Jesus as Lord. He cares for us and He is our friend, but He is also our Lord. We serve Him fully with all our heart, mind and soul. Our business is a ministry to build His Kingdom. He is the King of that Kingdom… Jesus is King of Kings and Lord of Lords. Our vision for unity is such that we bend knees together in unity to Jesus as Lord.

Twins Tours chooses to be a sustainable business rather than a donor supported ministry in order to be a source of stability and blessing to others. God provides miraculously for hundreds of ministries in Israel, but our desire is to be a source of stable economic provision for the ministry done by our staff as well as helping subsidize groups who cannot afford to come otherwise. In addition to subsidizing some Ministry Groups, Twins Tours will do once a year a Ministry Group completely free. The group only has to get to Israel and Twins Tours will cover the rest of the costs. Lastly, Twins Tours does familiarization tours for pastors which are also free to them. On familiarization tours, we invest in pastors for a week teaching them how to lead groups on the ground. These activities are only possible from the modest profits from the unsubsidized tours and the books we publish.

Another important part of the vision for Twins Tours is to send out ministers to bring the message of unity to others overseas. Currently Andre travels twice a year for 3-4 months and in the future, we envision, others will also be sent out.

Our Local Vision

Part of the vision of Twins Tours has always been to build up the local believing community by building bridges between Messianic Jews, Palestinian Christians, and the worldwide Church. A service tour is an excellent opportunity for your group to take part in the day-to-day ministries of the 'living stones' of this land, and to experience firsthand what God is doing today both in Israel and among the Palestinian Territories.

The Holy Land is larger than you think: Israel, Jordan & Egypt, Lebanon, Syria (Expansion to Turkey, Greece, Rome).

The heart of our vision is to be able to reach the forgotten Christian people especially in the heart of the west bank. Your presence is a big encouragement for the Christians in the west bank who are left and just to connect with them is a big deal. One example is with some of the ministry groups that partner with us, they help in running summer camps through the churches of the land for even simply visiting Christian homes for a dinner eating together at their homes and talking as well as also literally cleaning and painting their homes and villages as well working through the different municipalities.

Though these are little things, but it means a lot for the Christian people living in villages in the heart of the west bank and in the outskirts of Ramallah or one example the Zababdeh village near the city of Jenin. This is where almost no tourists get to and is away from the normal touristic sites. This will unite the west with the east and they will find simple people who want just to live a normal life, Twins Tours will prepare and help the people from the west how to be sensitive to their culture, as Palestinians have tight family relations. For example hugging is not encouraged, as well as when staying at their homes to have marine showers that is a very quick few minutes shower as water is scarce in the west bank and they don't get water every day, they will find out even the Palestinian Christians don't have much but they are very hospitable and serve fresh healthy food, coffee and tea. As they will be greeted with something to drink, and it is not nice at all to refuse the first drink, that will break the ice and not to ask immediately for the internet password when you first meet! Only listening to these people and to their daily struggles is something quite big for them as sometimes they are more open to foreigners. Twins Tours will help the west learn more about the Palestinian culture even help them in Olive harvesting for example as Palestinians are very good farmers, some folklore dance, etc. This way our pilgrims will experience more deeply not only the sites but as well the living stones of the land. It is not necessary to agree with all but try to understand each other.

The Twins Tours Team

Twins Tours office staff looks forward to meeting you and doing our best for your group to have the best experience in the Holy Land. We pray that while you are touring the land of the Bible, you will have a special encounter with the Holy Spirit. We are so excited that you were able to make this trip of a lifetime!

Andre & Marie Moubarak: *Andre* is the Co-founder and manager of Twins Tours and one of the main tour guides. *Marie* is the Director of Program & Partnership Development, and she has a heart to see visitors and pilgrims encounter the land and the people of Israel in a meaningful, integrity-filled way.

Tony & Sawsan Moubarak: *Tony* is the Co-Founder of Twins Tours and the main Tour Guide. He also helps manage the office when Andre is outside the country. *Sawsan* assists in accounting and manages supplier payments. Tony and Sawsan have 2 Children – 12 years old girl and 14 years old boy. Tony loves studying, reading, and writing so that he can teach the Word of God.

Setrag & Sylvia Shemmessian: *Setrag* is the Reservation Manager at Twins Tours, he deals with all the hotel bookings, site reservations, and daily emails and communications with all the suppliers. *Sylvia*, Setrag's wife, is the Accounting Manager and oversees all financial transactions. They have a newborn child almost 6 months old. Sylvia is Andre, Tony and Albert's cousin.

Albert Moubarak: *Albert* is the logistics manager in the office - he communicates with drivers and guides and supports the whole office. Albert and his wife, Rasha, have 3 children, two boys (6.5 yrs. old, 5.5 yrs. old), and one girl (4.5 yrs old).

Celesty Dabbagh: *Celesty* is the Media Projects Manager and a licensed Tour Guide with a deep love for the land of the Bible. When she is not on tours, she is at the Twins Tours office, creating physical and digital content to enhance and promote the business. Celesty is also Sawsan's niece.

Introduction

We invite you to join us on a pilgrimage to the Holy Land that will enrich and deepen your faith in the land where Jesus walked, died, and rose from the dead.

A trip to Israel is much more than just a vacation or a sightseeing trip; it is a life-transforming experience that will enable you and your group to encounter the land of the Bible and the ministry of Christ in its historical and geographical context.

Touring the Holy Land is an exciting way to visit Israel yourself and share the experience with others that you bring along, it is a vocation and ministry to which many people are called. As God leads, we hope that you prayerfully consider partnering with Twins Tours in leading a group to Israel.

We are here to walk you through the process, this book is made for you so do not hesitate to contact us if you need any assistance or have any questions that we did not address in this book.

We pray that you will enjoy reading this book and get ready and excited to visit Israel.

Twins Tours & Travel Team

I. Getting Started

1. **Your commitment to come.**
   One of the best ways to begin planning a trip to Israel with Twins Tours is to take a step of faith and to firmly decide to come yourself. When your friends, peers, and congregation see your commitment to this trip, people are more likely to respond enthusiastically and join you.

2. **Involve tour participants in a preparation study group.**
   Meeting regularly together will not only allow for everyone to get to know each other but will establish a strong spiritual foundation of prayer, learning, and discipleship within the group. We encourage our Tour Leaders to take a practical, hands-on role in the spiritual preparation of the group.

3. **Prayer Support.**
   We strongly suggest that you enlist prayer support from your home church during your preparation and your trip to Israel. We believe that having spiritual covering during a trip is an essential element in preparing your group for what the Lord has in store for them during their tour.

CHAPTER ONE

Planning & Promoting Your Tour to Israel

1. **Establish a leadership team, set goals, and enlist prayer support & spiritual covering**

Although you do not need any prior experience to lead a tour to Israel, you may want to enlist other individuals to help in coordinating the details of the trip. Establishing a leadership team of two or three people (especially if you are coming with a large group) can help drive the overall process and get the word out about the trip. This needs to include a group treasurer, who will handle the financial responsibilities for the trip from beginning to end, as well as a tour logistics administrator (getting from their home to the flight and all the way here to Israel).

The leadership team will ideally be responsible for:

- Communicating with potential tour participants.
- Sending promotional materials and information to churches or individuals.
- Creating and maintaining a list of people who have expressed interest in going to Israel (this is also helpful for organizing future trips to Israel).

- Coordinating regular meetings, prayer groups, or bible study for tour participants.

More importantly, we urge group leaders and participants to ask for prayer covering before, during, and after your tour. Prayer for strength, safety, and spiritual openness is crucial for the Holy Spirit to bring about life-changing growth.

2. Requesting the Tour Itinerary

This is where the 'nuts and bolts' planning of the tour begins. You will communicate your vision to Andre and Marie, the Program Director, and together customize a meaningful tour that accomplishes your goals.

3. Tour Price Quotation

After the tour itinerary is finalized, a Tour Price Quote will be given by Twins Tours. At this point, the Group Leader will have all the information necessary to plan and make decisions. As the quote is being developed, there are several factors to keep in mind.

- Prices are higher during Jewish holiday times.

- The number of participants will determine how many free places you receive.

- The prices quoted are for double occupancy (There is a single supplement fee for single occupancy rooms).

- The type of hotel will affect prices.

4. Reserving the Tour

The Tour Leader will then make a reservation with Twins Tours for the Tour, which will result in a final contract with a payment schedule. At this point, your flight details must be final.

5. **Prepare marketing materials**

Now that your Tour is designed, priced, and air portions are final, having up to date and effective marketing materials is an excellent way to promote it. You may find that setting up a simple website or Facebook page, or WhatsApp group is an easy and efficient way to distribute the trip's promotional materials and any other information.

6. **Reach out & register participants**

The upcoming Tour is now ready to be presented to potential participants in your circle of influence. This would include your church community, ministry partners, and friends as widely as possible by making announcements, short presentations, or hosting an informal 'Israel Orientation Meeting' to answer questions, show photos, and promote the tour, or even invite Andre to speak in your church about the trip.

7. **Payment Terms & Conditions**

- Payment Schedule: 50% of the entire amount should be transferred to our bank 60 days prior to arrival in Israel. Please add any additional sending fees. ($40 Varies with each bank & depends on the amount to be wired). For example, if the 50% down payment is $25,000, please send $25,000 + your banks' sending fees. Twins Tours will absorb the receiving fees on our end. The remaining balance should be transferred 3 weeks prior to arrival, again, adding any additional sending fees. After the transfers are made, immediately notify Twins Tours so we can confirm with our bank. Most international wire transfers take 2 days to one week to receive, depending on holidays, weekends, etc.

- Each payment will generate a receipt from Twins Tours with a final invoice showing all payments and any refunds, if applicable.

– Any additional costs accrued (such as an additional person added to the tour, etc.) can be paid in cash to Twins Tours upon arrival and a receipt will be given.

– Group Cancellation: If the group cancels less than 60 days prior to arrival, refunds are not guaranteed, and cancellation fees may be applied. However, if the cancellation is due to the unlikely event of war or national emergency, then Twins Tours will retain a small administration fee, and return the bulk of the monies paid. It will depend on each hotel's willingness to waive the cancellation fee.

– Individual Cancellation: If an individual participant cancels less than 14 days prior to arrival, then full refunds cannot be guaranteed, and cancellation fees may be applied. The situation will be evaluated on a case-by-case basis. Travel insurance that includes trip cancellation due to illness, injury or medical emergencies is highly advised.

– Tips: Tips must be given in cash (in three separate envelopes, labeled 'tour guide', 'bus driver' and 'hotel tips') with one set of envelopes per hotel. These monies go directly from the Tour Leader to the service providers and cannot be included in the wire transfer to Twins Tours & Travel Ltd. Customarily in Israel tips for tour guides, bus drivers and hotel workers are received independent of their salary.

Below is the tip chart to use when calculating tips.

	Guide/pp/day	Driver/pp/day	Hotel/pp/day
10-20 pax	$14	$9	$3
20-30 pax	$13	$8	$3
30-40 pax	$12	$7	$3
40-50 pax	$10	$5	$3

– Rates could be subject to change due to possible extreme fluctuations in the US dollar and fuel prices.

- Rates are based on these dates only; changes to tour dates may require re-pricing.

- Check-in to hotels on Saturdays are subject to late check-in procedures (up to three hours after the end of Shabbat). We will endeavor to schedule your tours to avoid these late check-in charges on Shabbat.

8. Tour Leader Responsibilities

Tour Leader Responsibilities – the Tour Leader is responsible for the team that he/she is bringing. This includes: having a packet of the following information with them at all times on the tour: a copy of each participants' passports, emergency contact info, a list of any prescription medications they take, and health insurance information for each participant in case of emergency. If there is a medical emergency or any other type of emergency, Twins Tours will assist the Tour Leader in making decisions on how to resolve the emergency.

9. Twins Tours Management Responsibilities

In the event of a security situation such as rioting, unrest or riots, route changes, accidents, weather conditions, etc. Twins Tours management is ultimately responsible for making the best decisions that might affect the itinerary and touring schedule. Our Tour Guides are in constant communication with law and security authorities about the safety of any location on the itinerary.

10. Tour Guide & Driver Working Hours

Tour Guides are restricted to work 9 hours/day. Any additional hours will be billed to the tour budget. Regarding buses, according to Israeli law, the daily limit is 200 kilometers and 9 hours. Extra fees will apply for any additional kilometers or hours.

11. **Administrative**

- Name tags – the Tour Leader will be responsible for printing and bringing name tags for each tour participant. On the back of the name tags, please include the names and phone numbers of the hotels, guides, etc. You can get this information from our office.

- Song sheets – many groups like to bring a small list of song sheets for the participants to use during times of worship.

- Devotional & Prayer Schedule – many groups often welcome the involvement of their participants and create a devotional and prayer schedule for each day of the tour. If you choose to do this, please have it organized before making the trip here.

- Journals – there is so much to see and learn in Israel and in such a short time! By the end of the trip, the days usually start to blur together. Twins Tours offers, for free, a "Twins Tours Study Reader," which includes journaling pages as well as pictures, maps, and additional study material. If you would like to have it before the trip, it is available in paperback on Amazon.com. Simply search for Twins Tour Study Reader, and you will find it.

- Wi-Fi – Most hotels will have areas with free Wi-Fi in the lobby, sometimes in the rooms. Buses have limited Wi-Fi. Also, there are some places in the country with limited cell phone reception, which affects the bus Wi-Fi system.

- Hair dryers in hotel rooms – Most hotels have hair dryers, guesthouses do not. So please keep this in mind as you plan your tour.

- Israeli cell phone SIM cards – We recommend that the Tour Leader have one for the Tour. Twins Tours can supply each group with one phone line for their time here to receive calls from your home country. We can assist you in obtaining the SIM cards. For tour participants who need to stay connected, it's advised to get an international calling or data plan from your home country organized before you arrive.

- Larger Groups – If your group is larger than forty participants, it is often helpful to have the group broken down into smaller groups with 'small group leaders'. This structure helps information get distributed quickly to the tour participants, and the small group leaders can help be on the lookout for problems the tour participants may encounter, such as a feeling of isolation, etc.

- Buses – Twins Tours have contracts with the two largest bus companies in Israel, with a selection of more than 450 vehicles – ranging from car-derived Mercedes vans for families that have 7 seats (like Mercedes Viano) to a van-based vehicle Mercedes minibus which has up to 16 passenger seats. There are also big buses that can seat up to 55 passengers. All the vehicles are brand new with wifi services.

- Audio Devices – for groups larger than 15 people, booking the wireless Whispers system helps make sure that every person in the group is equally able to hear the guide.

- Whatsapp Group – We recommend that the Tour Leader open a Whatsapp group for all the participants (and guide later) to stay in contact for updates and such during the tour.

- People with special needs – please advise us if any tour participants have mobility issues or special dietary needs; we have a supply of wheelchairs and crutches in our office in Jerusalem.

- Emergency and Medical Forms – The Tour Leader will be responsible for collecting emergency and medical contact forms. It is advised that they be kept together with the leader all throughout the tour in case of emergency.

Here are samples of what the forms look like.

HEALTH CONDITIONS

HEALTH CONDITIONS	
ARTHRITIS	
DIABETES	
CANCER	
STROKE	
SEIZURES	
LUNG PROBLEMS	
HEART PROBLEMS	
HIGH BLOOD PRESSURE	
KIDNEY PROBLEMS	
LIVER PROBLEMS	
JOINT REPLACEMENT	
DENTURES	
LENS IMPLANT	
PACEMAKER	
DEFIBRILLATOR	
HEARING AIDS	
OTHER	

PERSONAL INFORMATION

PERSONAL INFORMATION	
FULL NAME	
BIRTHDATE	
ADDRESS	
MOBILE PHONE	
PASSPORT #	
DOCTOR	
DOCTOR PHONE #	
INSURANCE	
INSURANCE #	
PHARMACY	
PHONE #	

ADVANCE DIRECTIVES I HAVE COMPLETED

ADVANCE DIRECTIVES I HAVE COMPLETED	
LIVING WILL	
POWER OF ATTORNEY - HEALTH	
NEITHER	
OTHER	

PAST SURGERIES	DATE

ALLERGIES	REACTION	DATE

MEDICATION	FOR	DOSE	FREQ.	DATE	PRESCRIBER	DATE

EMERGENCY CONTACT	HOW RELATED	MOBILE #	EMAIL ADDRESS

Tourism Terms Shortcuts

- Ap (Airport)
- Arr (Arrive)
- Itin (Itinerary)
- Quote (offer)
- Hrs (Hours)
- Trns (Transfer)
- LDC (Long Distance Coach – bus)
- W/L (Waiting list)
- Flt (Flight)
- Pax (Passenger)
- P.P (Per Pax)
- Htl (Hotel)
- TBA (To Be Announced)
- Divide (When group splits and leaves different times)
- Tkts (Tickets)
- F/C (First Class)
- T/L (Tour Leader)
- Grp (Group)
- AI (All Inclusive)
- HD (Halfday)
- FD (Full Day)
- BB (Bed and Breakfast)
- HB (Half Board) (no lunch)
- FB (Full Board)
- Trpl (Triple)
- Dbl (Double – 1 bed)
- Twin (2 beds)
- Sgl (Single room)
- Sgl Supplement – extra price for solo traveller
- RO (Room Only)
- O/N (Over Night)

FAQ'S

How far in advance should I begin planning a trip?

We suggest you allow yourself at least nine to twelve months before coming to Israel, although longer may be better, since you may find that you will need to promote the tour. Be aware it will take several weeks to negotiate with the airlines and book your flights. At that point, after your flights are confirmed, it is important to inform Twins Tours to finalize the tour program hotels and prices.

What does a Twins Tour include?

The price of the tour includes all of the basic expenses – Half board H/B (breakfasts & dinners at the hotels), trips, transportation, accommodation, and entrance fees.

What does a Twins Tour NOT include?

Travel insurance, optional trips, activities on free days, lunches, visa applications, personal fees, All Tips, and souvenir shopping.

Please note: Lunches can also be included, if desired, in most places, during the group touring days.

Do I need a visa?

Individuals holding passports from Europe & North America do not need a visa to visit Israel. Individuals from other countries need to check with an Israeli Consulate or Embassy to determine exact requirements. Here is a useful website to help you determine what Israel's visa requirements are:

http://mfa.gov.il/MFA/ConsularServices/Pages/Visas.aspx

Note that all visitors to Israel must arrive with a valid passport that does not expire within six months after your arrival in Israel.

When is the best time of year to visit?

It's up to you. Unless you specifically want to be in Israel for Christmas or Easter, you may want to schedule your trip at a time other than these busy holiday seasons. Weather conditions vary; from November to March, Israel has cool temperatures and some rain. (January and February have the highest rainfall). From June to August, temperatures are very warm, and the country is virtually rainless from April through October. A Twins Tours representative can help you decide on the best time for you and your group to visit.

Here is a helpful website to find out the Jewish holidays for each year:

https://www.hebcal.com/holidays/2015-2016

Is it safe to visit Israel?

People who have never been to Israel usually ask us this question – the answer is a clear and emphatic yes! The fact that millions of people visit Israel every year and return safe, fulfilled, inspired, and happy demonstrates how exaggerated news reports can be about Israel.

Ask someone who has been to Israel – then come and see for yourself.

What about bad news?

If there is negative news out of the Middle East, it is important to acknowledge it and communicate with the tour participants. If necessary, host a meeting to address concerns, review trip plans, and review Twins Tours safety precautions.

Twins Tours is available to do a Skype/Zoom/FaceTime meeting with the tour participants to discuss any of these issues. Please note that events in Syria or Iraq generally have little or no impact on daily life in Israel. State Department warnings you may have seen are usually for State Department employees. Twins Tours will adjust the tour itinerary to take into consideration any possible legitimate security concerns. This is why having a native Israeli guide and bus driver is to your advantage.

How much pocket money should I bring for tipping or other things?

Most currencies can be exchanged at the airport or by authorized money changers, which are available in most places your group will be visiting. Visa and MasterCard are accepted throughout the country; however, we recommend that you notify your bank and credit card company and inform them of your travel plans to avoid them potentially suspending your account due to irregular activity. Do not bring Travelers Checks, as they are accepted in very few places these days, and there will be little time to get them cashed during your tour.

Do I need travel health insurance?

The answer is YES. ☺ If your health insurance does not cover international travel, we strongly encourage participants to purchase a basic plan.

https://www.travelinsurancecenter.com

We are sure that you are all aware of this, but please double-check that every participant has travel insurance for the days in Israel, which includes coverage for medical emergency assistance during their trip. Please make sure every member has done it through your organization. In Israel, according to the law, this is a must.

It does not cost much – the alternative, to be without coverage during a medical emergency, can become very expensive if the participant does not have insurance.

They need to document that they have done it and send your organization all the information.

From our experience, each participant needs to carry a list of all their daily medications – including the names and the dosage – as well as any medications they are allergic to. In case of emergency, this list must be ready to give to the medical professionals. (pages 30-31 of this handbook provide a sample).

Do I need trip cancellation Insurance?

The answer is YES, again much recommended. Most travel health insurance companies have the option to add trip cancellation insurance.

How do I book my Flights?

- The minimum number of people required to travel together as a group is 10.

- You will need specific dates, city pairs – from and to – and group name. The sooner you book your flights, the better the option, rate, and availability will be.

- You can book as far in advance as 9 to 11 months out.

- Group bookings will require a deposit per person to hold a reservation, usually within 14 days of initial booking.

- Deposit is refunded after the trip is completed after deducting any penalties.

- 80 to 90% of the group travel/number has to be maintained 60-90 days prior to departure. This is called the utilization date.

- You can reduce your group number without penalty by this date.

- Final payment/full names/gender and ticketing is required 45-30 days prior to departure. Depending on the vendor/airline, payment can be made with a credit card or cheques/checks only.

- All contract terms and restrictions will be offered to the clients at the time of booking.

- We recommend contacting *Business Class Club* directly to set up your travel flights. (The contact information is listed below)

Nathan Essers
Personal Travel Agent
US +1 323 617-4697
AU +61 800 613 392
SG +65 3158 2690
8807 W. Pico Suite 207
Los Angeles, California
bookings@businessclassclub.com
www.businessclassclub.com/Enjoy-the-Club

CHAPTER TWO

Packing Checklist

TRAVEL DOCUMENTS:

☐ **Passport** – Please confirm that your passport expiration date is at least **six months** after your flight is scheduled to depart from Israel, and please make sure that your passport stays on your person always.

☐ One other form of personal ID, such as a driver's license.

☐ **Make a color photocopy of your passport and identification cards, to keep in a separate place from the real passport and ID cards.**

☐ Copy of Travel Itinerary.

☐ Copy of travel insurance document. **Please note – International Medical Insurance is mandatory for every traveler,** while trip cancellation insurance is optional.

☐ Luggage tags.

☐ Notify credit card companies and banks of the dates & countries of your travel.

☐ Leave credit cards except for the one that you might use at home. Credit cards are not widely accepted – they are generally for emergency situations only. VISA credit card is the most accepted internationally.

☐ It is best **not** to bring anything expensive with you on the trip (such as jewelry) – Modesty is observed in Israel and you do not want to make yourself a target.

☐ If desired, an international Data Plan for your smartphone. There is Wi-Fi available at hotels and restaurants. But there is no Wi-Fi available while touring.

CARRY-ON BAG ON THE AIRPLANE:

☐ Backpack or small personal item, such as a purse, for sightseeing.

☐ Medicine must be in a carry-on bag, and there must be enough medicine with each person that can last them for the entire trip. Also, every person should bring with him a list of all of the medications that he is taking, with the official prescribed medicine name and the dosage amount.

☐ Spare contact lenses or glasses.

☐ Clothing and personal necessities for 1-2 days & nights. Unfortunately, checked luggage occasionally gets lost or misplaced by the airlines and airports.

☐ Liquids must be in a quart-sized zip-lock bag. No liquids over 3 oz in your Carry-On bag, according to airport regulations.

☐ Electric Plug Adapters for Israel – please check the following link for further explanation about power converters and adapters: http://www.megavolt.co.il/Tips_and_info/visitor.html
Note: these travel adapters are available at CV's, Target, Walmart, etc. and at the airports.

CLOTHING & PERSONAL ITEMS IN CHECKED LARGE SUITCASE:

- ☐ Casual dress. Lightweight and loose-fitting clothing. Layers are best.
- ☐ Cargo pants are recommended.
- ☐ Windbreaker Jacket – Evenings can be cold and windy in Israel. It is a good idea to pack a sweater or lightweight jacket.
- ☐ 2 pairs of comfortable walking shoes – it is advisable to bring 2 pairs of comfortable walking shoes because if one pair gets wet and muddy, then you can wear the 2nd pair while the first pair dries in the hotel room. Please note that the streets and steps in Jerusalem are quite slippery so the shoes must have good treads.
- ☐ Sunglasses.
- ☐ Hat that will shade the face from the sun.
- ☐ Sunscreen – bring your own! Sunscreen is very expensive in Israel, and there are very limited options.
- ☐ Flip flops for the hotel bedrooms.
- ☐ For camel rides, it's required to have long pants and closed-toe shoes.
- ☐ Shorts for walking through the wet tunnel (Hezekiah's tunnel).
- ☐ Bathing Suit for the Dead Sea – advice: bring an inexpensive one, because the salts and minerals in the Dead Sea can be corrosive to some clothing materials. + recommended plastic bag (to wrap wet bathing suits after the Dead Sea).
- ☐ Water shoes – to use in the Dead Sea, Hezekiah's Tunnel, Jordan River.
- ☐ Water Clothes or a second swimming suit to use in the Jordan River. If people want to renew their baptismal vows by immersion in the Jordan River, the Yardenit Baptismal site will supply a white robe which becomes sheer/transparent when wet. So the person must be prepared by wearing appropriate clothing underneath this white robe. Please note that showers, changing rooms, and a towel are supplied by the Yardenit Baptismal Site.
- ☐ Toiletries + personal hygiene products. Washcloths, if desired.

☐ Umbrella if traveling during rainy season (October through March).

☐ Room for souvenirs on the way back!

MISCELLANEOUS suggested items to pack:

☐ A small personal journal for recording your memories.

☐ A small travel-size Bible, your favorite version to read at the Biblical sites, or during your personal devotion time on tour.

☐ Extra batteries, charging cords, and memory cards for your Camera.

☐ Snacks that will keep you healthy, if you get hungry between meals.

☐ Instant Coffee – the coffee in Israel's hotels is not very delicious. So, it is better if you bring your favorite instant coffee with you – Starbucks VIA Instant Coffee packs, or your favorite tea bags, or your favorite powdered packets for cold drinks.

☐ Coffee mugs with very secure lid to use in the bus – the bus driver will not allow any other kind of cups on the bus, like for example carton cups with plastic lids, glass mugs with no covers, etc.

☐ Your favorite Water Bottle to fill up at water fountains.

☐ Starting at least 2 weeks before the trip, hydrate as much as you can. Israel has a desert climate – which makes it very hot during the day, and in some places, all year long. If you are not properly hydrated before and during the visit, this will lead to dehydration and fatigue – bus drivers usually have cold water available on the bus for $1.00 per small bottle.

☐ Airplane/small travel pillow for long bus drives if desired.

☐ Aspirin or other nonprescription medications, including any motion sickness pills (you will be on a bus daily + a boat one day).

☐ We would suggest bringing along some of your favorite first aid supplies from the USA that you are familiar with using and consider to be essential. The guides carry a very basic first aid kit with mostly bandages, and we add to those first aid kits Imodium and Benadryl from the USA.

ITEMS **NOT** TO BRING:

- **Pocket Knives**: Israel considers pocket knives to be a Weapon, and carrying pocket knives on tour can cause serious security issues for both yourself and your tour guide.
- **Hair Dryers**: There are hair dryers in almost all the hotel rooms in Israel. So, you should not bring your own hair dryer. If there is no hair dryer in the room, there should be some in the reception that you can borrow. The electricity in Israel is 220-240 V, and it is not recommended to use a power converter for the hair dryer because it is dangerous and might cause an electricity blowout or even a fire in the hotel. If it is an absolute necessity to bring a curling iron, a straightener, a shaving machine etc., please make sure that they can be used internationally in other country's electrical systems.

CASH Money – Spending US Dollar Bills in Israel:

- Using US Dollars to pay for personal items and souvenirs in Israel is always accepted at Tourist Sites & Tourist Restaurants.
- Bring only Dollar Bills with you – Coins are not accepted at all.
- The dollar bills must be relatively new, with no marks or tears in the bill.
- Recommended to bring various kinds of dollar bills: $ 50, $ 20, $ 10, $ 5, $ 1.
- Sometimes the Israeli cashier will accept payment in dollar bills, but will only give change back to you in Israeli money (shekels).
- It is possible to change money to Israeli Shekels using Official ATM's like the ones that are in the airport – they accept VISA Debit cards. You can also ask the tour guide that is with you where is the best place to change some money to Israeli Shekels.

Clothing Rules in the Holy Land

Each day, the Tour Guide who travels with your group will give you instructions about appropriate clothing for the next day's activities. Please follow the rules to ensure that you can enjoy every moment of the scheduled activities with the tour group.

Modest dress is mandatory at churches and other Holy sites. This means that everyone's knees and shoulders must be well covered up. Very little skin showing. No shorts, no tank tops, no sleeveless shirts, no low cut shirts that show cleavage, and definitely no tights/leggings as pants. On hot days, some women get around this modest dress restriction by wearing sleeveless shirts at the regular sites and in the bus, and then just throwing on a shirt or shawl or scarf around their shoulders before entering a holy site. But the rules are strict about shorts – the religious doorkeepers will forbid entry to any person who is wearing shorts. Capri pants that show the lower calf and ankle are acceptable for women.

If you go on top of the Temple Mount, near the Al Aqsa Mosque, because it is a Muslim Holy Site, women may feel more comfortable by covering their heads/ hair with a scarf because it makes them more socially acceptable by the Muslim cultural norms.

In Jewish Holy Sites, such as the Western Wall, it is mandatory for men to cover their heads. Either they can wear their own hat, or the Jewish religious doorkeeper will give them a paper kippah (yarmulke) to cover the top of their head.

In Christian Holy Sites, especially inside churches, it is mandatory for men to uncover their heads – men are forbidden to wear hats inside churches.

In east Jerusalem and the West Bank, it is not culturally appropriate to show very much skin. Please try to dress modestly if your hotel is located in those regions.

CHAPTER THREE

About the Country

General info

Weather:

	Jerusalem	Tel Aviv	Haifa	Safed	Tiberias	Dead Sea
Jan.	43-54° F 6-12° C	48-66° F 9-19° C	46-63° F 8-17° C	37-50° F 3-10° C	48-65° F 9-18° C	53-69° F 12-21° C
March	47-61° F 8-16° C	51-68° F 11-20° C	47-70° F 8-21° C	43-55° F 6-13° C	51-72° F 11-22° C	60-78° F 16-26° C
July	67-83° F 19-28° C	70-87° F 21-31° C	68-86° F 20-30° C	65-84° F 18-29° C	72-98° F 22-37° C	83-102° F 28-39° C
Nov	54-66° F 12-19° C	55-75° F 13-24° C	56-73° F 13-23° C	54-66° F 12-19° C	59-78° F 15-26° C	65-80° F 18-27° C

Time Difference: 7 hours ahead of Eastern Standard Time

Currency conversion:

1 US Dollar = 3.5 ILS

1 British Pound = 4.4 ILS

1 Euro = 3.9 ILS

Israel

Capital: Jerusalem

Official Languages: Hebrew and Arabic

Government: Parliamentary Democracy (120 in Knesset like the Great Assembly of the 2nd Temple Period)

Population: 9.1 million (75% Jews, 21% Arab, 4% other)

Currency: New Israeli Shekel (ILS/NIS)

Major Religions: Judaism, Islam, Christianity

Industry: Technology, pharmaceuticals, tourism, manufacturing, military

National Bird: Hoopoe

National Flower: Cyclamen Persicum

Palestinian Territories / West Bank

Capital: Ramallah but with aim for Jerusalem

Official Language: Arabic

Government: Parliamentary Democracy

Population: 5 million (West Bank 3.2 million, Gaza Strip 1.8 million)

Currency: New Israeli Shekel (ILS / NIS)

Major Religions: Islam, Christianity

Industry: Tourism, quarrying, small family businesses

CHAPTER FOUR

Cross-Cultural Info

Technology:

The creative and diverse Israelis have strong determination to push past the boundaries of possibility and facing challenges head-on. It is no wonder that Israel is now the world's leading innovation country with the highest number of startups in the world, earning it the title "Start-Up Nation".

Religions:

This is the center of the world's three great monotheistic faiths: The Promise Land of milk and honey to the Jews, the scene of Christ's Ministry, Crucifixion and Resurrection to the Christians, and to the Muslims, the site of the prophet Mohammad's night ascent to heaven.

Location:

Israel is located in the Middle East, along the eastern coastline of the Mediterranean Sea, bordered by Lebanon, Syria, Jordan, and Egypt. It lies at the junction of three continents: Europe, Asia, and Africa.

Geography:

Long and narrow in shape, the country is about 290 miles (470 km) in length and 85 miles (135 km) in width at its widest point. Although small in size, Israel encompasses the varied topographical features of an entire continent – ranging from forested highlands to fertile green valleys to mountainous deserts. Approximately half of the country's land area is semi-arid.

Climate:

Israel's climate is characterized by much sunshine, with a rainy season from November to April. Total annual precipitation ranges from 20-30 inches (50-70 cm) in the north to about an inch (2.5 cm) in the far south. Regional climatic conditions vary considerably: hot, humid summers and mild, wet winters on the coastal plain; dry, warm summers and moderately cold winters, with rain and occasional light snow, in the hill regions; hot, dry summers and pleasant winters in the Jordan Valley; and semi-arid conditions, with warm to hot days and cool nights, in the south.

Flora and Fauna:

The rich variety of Israel's plant and animal life reflects its geographical location as well as its varied topography and climate. Over 500 kinds of birds, some 200 mammal and reptile species, and 2,600 plant types (150 of which are endemic to Israel) are found within its borders. Over 150 nature reserves and 65 national parks, encompassing nearly 400 square miles (almost 1,000 sq. km), have been established throughout the country.

Water:

The scarcity of water in the region has generated intense efforts to maximize the use of the available supply and to seek new resources. In the 1960s, Israel's freshwater sources were joined in an integrated grid whose main artery, the National Water Carrier, brings water from the north and center to the semi-arid south. Ongoing projects for utilizing new sources include cloud seeding, recycling of sewage water, and the desalination of seawater.

Population:

Israel is a country of immigrants. Since its inception in 1948, Israel's population has grown five-fold. Its 9.1 million inhabitants comprise a mosaic of people with varied ethnic backgrounds, lifestyles, religions, cultures, and traditions. Today Jews comprise some 76% of the country's population, while the country's non-Jewish citizens, mostly Arabs, number about 24%.

Lifestyle:

About 92% of Israel's inhabitants live in some 200 urban centers, some of which are located on ancient historical sites. About 5% are members of unique rural cooperative settlements – the kibbutz and the moshav.

> *Moshav:* A unique type of cooperative farmer's village invented in Israel in the early 1900s. The members of the Moshav enjoy relatively large economic autonomy while still benefiting from communal assistance.

> *Kibbutz:* A unique form of collective community based on socialist ideology and the promotion of the Zionist idea. Members of a Kibbutz are usually a close-knit group with shared property, labor, and the provision for all the needs of its members.

Main Cities:

1. Jerusalem, Israel's capital (population 900,000), has stood at the center of the Jewish people's national and spiritual life since King David made it the capital of his kingdom some 3000 years ago. Today it is a flourishing, vibrant metropolis, the seat of the government, and Israel's largest city.

2. Tel Aviv-Yafo (population 440,000), which was founded in 1909 as the first Jewish city in modern times, is today the center of the country's industrial, commercial, financial, and cultural life.

3. Haifa (population 280,000), a known coastal town since ancient times, is a major Mediterranean port and the industrial and commercial center of northern Israel.

4. Be'er Sheva (population 207,000), named in the Bible as an encampment of the patriarchs, is today the largest urban center in the south. It provides administrative, economic, health, education and social services for the entire southern region.

System of Government:

Israel is a parliamentary democracy with legislative, executive, and judicial branches. The head of state is the president, whose duties are mostly ceremonial and formal; the office symbolizes the unity and sovereignty of the state. The Knesset, Israel's legislative authority, is a 120-member unicameral parliament which operates in plenary session and through 15 standing committees. Its members are elected every four years in universal nationwide elections. The government (cabinet of ministers) is charged with administering internal and foreign affairs. It is headed by a prime minister and is collectively responsible to the Knesset.

Education and Science:

School attendance is mandatory from age five, and free through age 18. Almost all three-years-olds and four-year-olds attend some kind of preschool program.

Israel's institutions of higher education include universities, offering a wide range of subjects in science and humanities, and serving as research institutions of worldwide reputed colleges providing academic courses and vocational schools. The country's high level of scientific research and development and the application of R&D compensate for the country's lack of natural resources.

Health:

The National Health Insurance Law, in effect from January 1995, provides for a standardized basket of medical services, including hospitalization, for all residents of Israel. All medical services continue to be supplied by the country's four health care organizations. Life expectancy is 82.2 years for women and 78.5 years for men; the infant mortality rate is 4 per 1,000 live births. The ratio of physicians to population and the number of specialists compare favorably with those in most developed countries.

Social Welfare:

The social service system is based on legislation which provides for workers' protection and a broad range of national and community services, including care of the elderly, assistance for single parents, programs for children and youth, adoption agencies, as well as prevention and treatment of alcoholism and drug abuse.

The National Insurance Institute provides all permanent residents (including non-citizens) with a broad range of benefits, including unemployment insurance, old-age pensions, survivors' benefits, maternity grants and allowances, child allowances, income support payments and more.

Economy :
- GDP $354 billion
- ($39,100 per capita)
- Exports, goods, and services $60.6 billion
- Imports, goods, and services $66.8 billion

Industry:
Israel's industry concentrates on manufacturing products with a high added value that are primarily based on technological innovation. These include medical electronics, agrotechnology, telecommunications, computer hardware and software, solar energy, food processing and, fine chemicals.

Agriculture:
Israel's agricultural successes are the result of a long struggle against harsh, adverse conditions and of making maximum use of scarce water and arable land. Today, agriculture represents some 2.5% of GNP and 2.2% of exports. Israel produces 93% of its own food requirements, supplemented by imports of grain, oil seeds, meat, coffee, cocoa, and sugar, which are more than offset by the wide range of agricultural products for export.

Foreign Trade:
Trade is conducted with countries on six continents. Some 49% of imports and 33% of exports are with Europe, boosted by Israel's free trade agreement with the EU (concluded in 1975). A similar agreement was signed with the United States (1985), whose trade with Israel accounts for 12.4% of Israel's imports and 38% of its exports.

Culture:

With thousands of years of history, the ingathering of the Jews from over 70 countries, a society of multi-ethnic communities living side by side, and an unending flow of international input via satellite and cable – have contributed to the development of an Israeli culture which reflects worldwide elements while striving for an identity of its own. Cultural expression through the arts is as varied as the people themselves, with literature, theater, concerts, radio and television programming, entertainment, museums, and galleries for every interest and taste.

Gender:

People in the Middle East often greet each other with a kiss – men to men and women to women, but rarely to the opposite gender unless they are family. Purity is highly valued. While most Americans are accustomed to hugging, this is rare in the Holy Land. Public displays of affection, in general, may be different or even non-existent. In some areas, men and women do not socialize publicly – making prolonged eye contact with someone from the opposite gender is even considered inappropriate.

Languages:

The official languages of the country are Hebrew and Arabic, but in the country's streets, many other languages can be heard. Hebrew, the language of the Bible, long restricted to liturgy and literature, was revived a century ago, accompanying the renewal of Jewish life in the Land.

Israeli Cuisine:

From European dishes to the Middle Eastern and Mediterranean, Israel's rich diversity is strongly represented by its cuisine as well. A big part of the daily meal includes delicacies such as locally grown fruits and vegetables, olive oil, hummus, tahini, and more.

Due to religious dietary laws such as the Jewish Kosher laws and Muslim Hallal laws, pork is not common in Israel (though it can still be found in more Christian or secular places). Kosher laws also restrict combining meat and dairy products in many restaurants and most hotels.

Entertainment:

Entertainment in Israel, much like its population, is very diverse, yet still manages to be distinguished as its own entity. From live music and concerts to operas, dances, and sketch comedies, it brings people from different backgrounds together. Theaters perform Hebrew remakes of world-famous plays as well as original content. Cinemas and TV enjoy Hebrew subtitles over Hebrew dubbing (unless for preschoolers). Creative Israelis also brought forth original movies and shows both in Hebrew and Arabic that are loved world-wide today.

Shopping:

Shopping is a popular pastime in Israel from luxurious malls to crowded and lively marketplaces in every major city. We recommend visiting the Mahne Yehuda farmers market in Jerusalem for a local authentic shopping experience – welcome to the "Walmart" of Jerusalem!

Bethlehem – the city of Jesus' birth – also has many souvenir shops. You can find everything from gold jewelry sets, to oil lamps, to olive-wood statues and other artifacts. Name any biblical character or animal, and there is an impressive olive-wood statue for you! Favorites included Samson pushing the pillars, David slaying Goliath and, of course, Nativity scenes of every shape, size and price—from a few bucks to a few thousand.

Sports:
From skiing on Mt Hermon to scuba diving in the Red Sea, Israelis enjoy a variety of sports for hobbies as well as professions. Soccer (called Football / Kadoor Regel) just edges basketball as the most popular sport in Israel, with teams competing nationally as well as internationally. Most notable are Maccabi Haifa and Betar Jerusalem. When it comes to basketball, Maccabi Tel Aviv's very own Omri Caspi became the first Israeli to join the NBA. Israel also prides itself on its Olympic success, and even hosts its own version called the Maccabiah Games for Jews from all over the world every four years – one of only seven worldwide competitions recognized by the International Olympic Committee.

Soldiers:
The IDF, founded in 1948, ranks among the most battle-tested armed forces in the world, having had to defend the country in six major wars. The IDF's security objectives are to defend the sovereignty and territorial integrity of the State of Israel, deter all enemies, and curb all forms of terrorism that threaten daily life.

Compulsory Service: All eligible men and women are drafted at age 18. Men serve for three years, women for two years. Deferments may be granted to qualified students at institutions of higher education. New immigrants may be deferred or serve for shorter periods of time, depending on their age and personal status on entering the country.

Reserve Duty: Upon completion of compulsory service, each soldier is assigned to a reserve unit and may serve up to the age of 51.

Career Military Service: Veterans of compulsory service meeting current IDF needs may sign up as career officers or NCOs. The career service constitutes the command and administrative backbone of the IDF. Graduates of officers' or pilots' schools or special military technical schools are required to sign on for periods of career service.

CHAPTER FIVE

Holidays and Festivals

Holidays are very confusing in this part of the world. Not only are there secular, Jewish, Christian, and Islamic holidays, but the dates they fall on are related to the Hebrew lunisolar calendar, the solar Gregorian Calendar, plus a sighting of the new moon at Mecca. And not only that, but various Christian denominations celebrate key events on different days.

Jewish Feasts

The Jewish calendar is both lunar and solar. It follows the sun for the year and the moon for the month. Every three years is a leap year, and one month is added to keep the feasts and festivals as close as possible to the seasons as in Scriptures. The Sabbath is very important to the Jewish people and life in Israel in general. In most places around the country and especially in Jerusalem, Friday afternoon to Saturday evening, everything shuts down, including transportation. In Jewish tradition, the day begins at sunset.

Rosh Hashanah: *The Jewish New Year / Feast of Trumpets* – Trumpets are blown to remind people to repent of their sins as the Day of Atonement is approaching. Though a solemn holiday, it is celebrated with apples and honey for a "prosperous and sweet" new year.

Yom Kippur: *The Day of Atonement* – Holiest day of the year for the Jewish People and a national day of fasting. This tradition goes back to Biblical times of the Tabernacle, where once a year on Yom Kippur, the High Priest entered the Holy of Holies to atone for the people's sins.

Sukkot: *The Feast of Tabernacles* – A weeklong holiday that comes five days after Yom Kippur. It celebrates the gathering of the harvest and commemorates God's protection and provision for the Israelites after they left Egypt. The festival of Sukkot is one of the three pilgrimage feasts and is celebrated by dwelling in a foliage-covered booth (sukkah) and by waving four species of plants – palm, myrtle, willow, and citron.

Simchat Torah: *The Rejoicing of the Law* – a joyous celebration that marks the end and beginning of the cycle of public Torah readings.

Hanukkah: *Feast of Lights* – An eight-day Jewish celebration of the Maccabees' victory over the Greeks in 165 BC. To remember the miraculous provision of oil for the light in the temple, Hanukkah is celebrated by daily lighting a new candle on a Hanukkiah (9-branched Menorah) and eating food deep-fried in oil, such as the sufganiyot (jelly doughnuts).

Purim: *The Festival of Lots* – Celebrates the bravery of a Jewish girl who became queen and saved her people, the Jews, in ancient Persia. This bizarre holiday is celebrated by fancy dress-ups (to allude to the hidden features in the story), much feasting, and loud, interactive reading of the Book of Esther in the synagogues.

Pessah: *Passover* – Commemorates God's Deliverance of Israel out of Egypt. A perfect lamb was slain, and its blood was painted on the doorposts, all so that the punishment of the Lord will "pass over" the homes of the children of Israel. The event is celebrated with a special family meal called the Seder by which the story is told. Another Passover tradition is cleaning the house from any yeast, and bread is replaced with a cracker called Matzah. Passover is one of the three pilgrimage feasts.

Shavuot: *Festival of Weeks / Pentecost* – it is celebrated 50 days after Passover as the day in which God gave the Torah to Moses on Mount Sinai. Shavuot is one of the three pilgrimage feasts. Today, it is customary to stay up all night reading the Torah.

Lag B'Omer: *The 33rd day of the Omer* – the Omer is the 49 days between Passover (Pessach) and Pentecost (Shavuot). The holiday celebrates a break in the dreadful plague at the time of Rabbi Akiva. Rabbi Shimon Bar Yochai (Rashbi, an important Jewish mystic) is also said to have died on that day, which in Jewish tradition means his life purpose was fulfilled and, therefore, a day of joy. Lag B'Omer is celebrated by building bonfires, playing sports, and enjoying picnics.

Tisha B'av: *the Ninth of Av* (Hebrew month) – is an annual fast day of communal mourning over a number of disasters in Jewish history, primarily the destruction of the First and Second Temples in Jerusalem.

Israeli Secular Holidays

Yom Hashoah: *(Holocaust Memorial)* National remembrance day for the tragedy of the Holocaust in which 6 million Jews were murdered.

Yom Hazikaron: *(Remembrance Day)* National remembrance day for all the soldiers who lost their lives defending the State of Israel. A siren is sounded, and all Israeli citizens stop what they are doing and stand firm in silence to honor the lives lost.

Yom Haatzmaut: *(Independence Day)* The day of Israel, a celebration of the Declaration of the State of Israel on the 14th of May 1948. The celebration day changes each year as it follows the Hebrew calendar (in this case, the 5th of Iyar), and it is always preceded by the Day of Remembrance for the fallen soldiers.

Yom Yerushalayim: *(Jerusalem Day)* commemoration of the reunification of Jerusalem after the Six-Day War in 1967.

Christian Feasts

These Festivals are celebrated on different dates by Eastern Orthodox and western churches (Latin, Roman Catholic, and Protestant, etc.). For Christians, Sunday is a special holy day, and so, many Christians do not work on Sundays as they would be with their families at church. (Touristic places are generally still open though).

Christmas: 25th of December or 7th of January. With Christianity being a minority, it is less common to find Christmas symbols around Israel than in many other countries. However, major religious centers such as Nazareth, Bethlehem, and the Old City of Jerusalem experience festivities that bring the story of the Nativity to life! Lighting up the Christmas tree in different towns, Christmas markets, concerts, plays and more, Christmas in the Holy Land is like you have never seen it before!

Lent: 40 days of fasting observed by many churches in preparation for Easter. It begins on Ash Wednesday, a holy day for prayer and fasting for repentance and ends the day before Easter Sunday. The number 40 is related to Jesus fasting in the desert for 40 days.

Palm Sunday: Palm Sunday marks the beginning of the Holy Week and celebrates the arrival of Jesus in Jerusalem. Today, Palm Sunday is celebrated with a procession in the footsteps of Jesus from Mount of Olives and through the Old City. Families from many denominations join in with their best attire and wave palm branches (or crosses made from palm leaves) on this joyful event led by marching bands. Palm Sunday and Easter are not only movable days but multiple in this region – the day in some years may be Palm Sunday for some people and Easter Sunday for others.

Good Friday: the day Jesus was crucified, it is commemorated by some churches by following in his footsteps from Gethsemane to Golgotha to be crucified. Thousands of pilgrims follow the path called Via Dolorosa ("Way of the Pain") while holding crosses.

Holy Saturday: crowds gather at the Holy Sepulchre church to witness the miracle of the Holy Fire being lit, and the light is distributed to all and sent all over the world to light the churches for the next year.

Easter Sunday: The Tomb is empty and the Savior is risen! Easter, also known as Pascha, is celebrated all over Israel with the highlight being in Jerusalem. It is celebrated with family visits, egg hunts, and church services, but the highlight for Protestants is the sunrise service at the Garden Tomb. Eastern and Western churches usually celebrate on different days, yet it has happened where they coincide on the same day. Easter and the Jewish Passover often overlap as well as Jesus' death and resurrection occurred during Passover.

Muslim Holidays

The Islamic calendar began on the 16th July 622 AD, the date of the Hijra, and follows a lunar calendar. For Muslims, Friday is the holiest day, and so many local areas with generally Muslim population close down on Fridays.

Ras Elsana al Hijriya: *(The Hijri New Year / Islamic New Year)* – The years in Islam started counting in 622 AD on the day Muhammad and his followers emigrated from Mecca to Medina – known as the Hijra.

The Hijri calendar is a lunar calendar with 354/355 days a year and consists of 12 months.

Mawlid al Nabi: *(Birth of the Prophet)* – Commemorates the birth of Prophet Muhammad and is celebrated in a carnival manner with large street processions and reading the stories of Muhammad's life.

Lailat al Miraj: One of the most significant events in the Muslim calendar. This festival celebrates the night journey and ascent of prophet Muhammad. According to Muslim tradition, Muhammad was taken from Mecca to Jerusalem on a mythical winged creature called Buraq, and from there, he ascends to heaven where he is validated as the last and final prophet.

Ramadan: The ninth month of the Islamic calendar and observed by Muslims worldwide as the month of fasting. It is remembered as the month in which the Quran was given to Muhammad. According to Muslims, during Ramadan, the gates of heaven are opened, and gates of Hell are closed. As one of the Five Pillars of Islam, all Muslims fast from sunrise to sunset and celebrate with feasts each night during this month.

Eid Al Fitr: *(Festival of Breaking Fast)* – Just as its name implies, it celebrates the end of the Ramadan fast with three days of festivities.

Eid El-Adha: *(Festival of Sacrifice)* – This festival celebrates Abraham's willingness to sacrifice his son, Ishmael. It is celebrated with gatherings and feasts, and it is customary to eat an abundance of meat during these three days. Eid Al Adha coincides with the completion of the Hajj – the annual pilgrimage to Mecca.

CHAPTER SIX

Israel's Diverse Population

Secular Jew
They hold on to their identity as a Jewish culture mixed in with modern society, without the faith of their ancestors. Makeup over 40% of the Jewish population.

Ultra-Orthodox Jew
Jews that are pro-religious coercion and emphasize studying the Torah and Talmud. Some of them do not recognize the State of Israel as legitimate and do not join the IDF.

Arab Muslim
18% of the population in Israel.

National Religious Jew
Recognize the modern state as a legitimate entity yet still desire for Israel to become a religious state.

Jewish Believer in Jesus
Also known as Messianic Jews, they preserve the Jewish culture yet accept Jesus as their Lord and Savior. Around 20,000.

Arab Israelis
Arabs who own an Israeli ID. Most self-designate themselves as Palestinians by nationality and Israeli by citizenship, while others prefer "Israeli Arab."

Arab Christian

Around 175,000 Arab Christians live in Israel. They are from a variety of denominational backgrounds such as Baptist, Roman Catholic, Greek Orthodox, Anglican, Baptist, Melchite, and others.

Muslim Background Believer (MBB)

Over 300 in Israel. They are usually not publicly announced as they are in danger of their neighbors and families.

Armenians

Part of the Armenian Diaspora, around 800 Armenians live in the Armenian quarter of the Old City and 10,000 in Israel.

Druze

An offshoot of Islam whose people have a secret religion and are loyal to the State of Israel. 104,000 in population, most in northern Israel.

Palestinian Muslim

Makeup 99% of the Palestinian Authority areas.

Palestinian Christian

Only 1% of the Palestinian population. Leaving the land because of Islamic persecution.

Palestinian Jew

Jews that lived in the land before the foundation of the State of Israel in 1948 and speak Arabic fluently.

Bedouin

Nomadic Arab tribes who mostly live in the desert and have the highest fertility rate in the world. Many of them volunteer in the IDF.

Samaritans

Israel's smallest religious minority and own an Israeli ID. Assimilated descendants of the Assyrians and residents of the district of Samaria who consider themselves the original Jews and recognize their own version of the Pentateuch plus the book of Joshua.

Refugees & Asylum Seekers
From Sudan, the Philippines, China, Kosovo, Thailand, even Christian Lebanese soldiers from the 1981 war.

Immigrant
Jews from all over the world who made Aliyah to Israel, 37% of the population.

Jerusalem Syndrome Sufferer
People from either Jewish or Christian backgrounds who see themselves as prophetic biblical figures when visiting Jerusalem.

Expatriate
Mostly found in Jerusalem.

CHAPTER SEVEN

Money Matters in Israel

Name

The Israeli currency is called the **shekel** (plural: shekalim). The shekel is divided into 100 agorot (singular: agora). The word *shekel* is derived from the ancient biblical currency of the same name.

Prices are often written in English as "xxx NIS," which is an abbreviation of "New Israeli Shekel," the full name of the currency. You will also see the symbol ₪ used.

Changing Money

You will get a better rate of exchange if you change money once you arrive in Israel rather than if you buy them abroad.

There are a couple of change places in the airport if you are desperate for cash when you arrive, but you will get a better rate outside of the airport.

There are plenty of ATMs (called caspomat in Hebrew) where you can withdraw money using your regular credit card (see credit card usage section below). The machines will all give you the option of conducting the transaction in English, so don't worry about not understanding the instructions.

There are also many change places in the main tourist areas. Make sure to have your passport on you as a security check if you are going to be exchanging foreign currency for shekels.

Avoid changing money in hotels as you will get a poorer rate than at a change place or from the ATM.

Some shops, restaurants, attractions in tourist areas will accept dollars as well as shekels, but make sure you are not overpaying by using dollars rather than shekels.

Using a Credit Card in Israel

Credit cards are widely accepted in Israel.

Before you travel, notify your credit card company that you will be traveling abroad to avoid having fraud alerts or holds being put on your account, which could make taking out money very tricky.

ATMs are widespread, and many will accept foreign credit cards, making it easy to withdraw money rather than having to carry around a lot of cash either in dollars or shekels.

Make sure you check how much you will be charged for foreign transactions before you travel to ensure you know how much each withdrawal will cost.

Coins

Shekel coins come in denominations of 10 and 50 agorot and 1, 2, 5 and 10 shekels.

10 agorot is worth very little, about $0.03

50 agorot is worth approximately $0.14

1 shekel is worth approximately $0.29

2 shekels is worth approximately $0.58

5 shekels is worth approximately $1.44

10 shekels is worth approximately $2.88

Bank Notes

Israeli banknotes are available in denominations of 20, 50, 100 and 200 shekalim. The different values are printed in different colors to make it easy to distinguish between them.

Did you know that a shekel was a coin that represented a claim on a weight of barley held in the city warehouse, This coin weighed the equivalent of about 180 grains of barley (approximately 11 grams). The Hebrew word shekel is based on the Semitic verbal root for "weighing."

20 Shekel Note [RED]
Worth approximately $5.60.

The 20 shekel note features the shoreline of the Sea of Galilee as well as Rachel the Poetess against a background of palm tree branches.

50 Shekel Note [GREEN]
Worth approximately $14.

The 50 shekel note features a Corinthian column and the Russian-born poet Shaul Tchernichovsky against a background of a citrus tree and its fruits.

100 Shekel Note [YELLOW]
Worth approximately $28.

The 100 shekel note features deer as well as the renowned poet Leah Goldberg against a background of almond tree blossoms.

200 Shekel Note [BLUE]
Worth approximately $56.

The 200 shekel note features moonlit flora as well as the poet Nathan Alterman set against a background of autumn leaves.

II. While in Israel

- **Stay in touch** – Before you come, consider creating a list of people (with their contact information) that would like to receive regular updates from the group while in Israel. This is especially important for those who will be praying for the group so that they can know how and when to pray.

- **Take lots of photos and videos** – make sure that someone on the trip has a good quality camera to photograph and record the trip highlights.

- **Establish contact** – Even if your itinerary does not include a meeting with a local ministry or congregation, we encourage everyone to reach out and talk to believers and unbelievers living in the Holy Land. Personal connection with local believers can be an eye-opening encounter.

CHAPTER EIGHT

Sample Itinerary

12 days/11 Nights Pilgrimage in Israel

We will travel through the land, from coast to desert to mountains, visit the places where important Biblical events took place, and dig deep into the Scriptures in their original context to learn about God's faithfulness to His people— in the past, present, and future. Our tour includes sites from the Old and New Testaments as well as the history of modern Israel.

Day 1 – Arrival In The Land of Promise

Twins Tours representative to introduce our guide and bus driver for the trip will meet the group. From the airport, we will travel to our hotel on the coast.

Jaffa / Tel Aviv – Tour the Old City Port of Jaffa and explore the home of Simon the Tanner, a light to the gentiles. Drive through Tel Aviv to study about the modern state of Israel.

Dinner & (1) Overnight at the Mediterranean Coast

Day 2 – The Coastal Plain: Jews, Gentiles & The Messiah

Check out from hotel

Travel along the Via Maris, the ancient international coastal highway. Theme: Pagan nations encounter the God of Israel – Romans, Phoenicians, Canaanites, and Egyptians.

Caesarea Maritima – Gateway of Rome to the east – Springboard of Christianity to the west. Explore the magnificent port city & man-made harbor, built by King Herod to honor Roman Emperor Augustus Caesar, later becoming the seat of Roman governors in 1st c AD. Here the apostle Peter proclaimed the Gospel of Jesus Christ to a god-fearing Roman centurion named Cornelius — and the whole gentile household was baptized by the Holy Spirit *(Acts 10)*. Here a prisoner named Paul shared his conversion testimony before royalty *(Acts 26)*, and the port of Caesarea became the base for mission trips across the Mediterranean Sea.

Mt. Carmel – Elijah vs. Priests of Baal during the reign of King Ahab & Queen Jezebel.

Situated high above the Jezreel Valley, Mt Carmel is where the prophet Elijah defeated the prophets of Baal *(1 Kings 18)*, upon whom God sent the fire down from Heaven. The church at Muhraka is a perfect place to recount the biblical events. The rooftop observation point provides a panoramic view of the fertile Jezreel Valley and surrounding hills – Nazareth, Mt. Tabor, Mt. Moreh, Mt. Gilboa – *"a land of mountains and valleys that drinks rain from heaven" (Deut 11:11)*.

Megiddo – the Plain of Armageddon. Continuing along the ancient highway that connected Egypt to Mesopotamia, we drive by the most important gateway city of Canaan – Megiddo. Many pharaohs, kings, and emperors have fought bloody battles in the Jezreel Valley to control this strategic pass by Mt Carmel. No wonder this will be the location of the final battle of Armageddon (Revelation). If time permits, we will explore the layers of civilization on this historic tel – including Solomon's city gates, a Canaanite altar, and a hidden water tunnel.

Dinner & (4) Overnights in Tiberias hotel or a kibbutz guest house along the lakeshore.

Day 3 – The Lower Galilee: The Word Became Flesh and Dwelled Among Us

Drive east through the Lower Galilee. This is the same route that Jesus traveled on.

Mt. Arbel – overlook the Sea of Galilee region, where Jesus spent most of his 3-year public ministry, as recorded in the Gospels. Mt. Arbel is first mentioned in *Hosea 10:14*

Sepphoris – is a village and an archeological site located in the central Galilee built as the capital of Galilee in the 1st century and believed to be the working place of Joseph as it is within walking distance from Nazareth.

Nazareth is the place of Jesus's childhood *(Luke 1 & 2)*, and today has the largest concentration of Christians in Israel. Its first importance is for angel Gabriel's announcement to Mary that she will bear God's son.

We will briefly visit the **Church of the Annunciation**, where the Word became Flesh, and appreciate how Mary is revered by cultures all around the world. Underneath the church are ancient dwelling places, and nearby is a cemetery with a rolling stone from the 1st century AD.

Nazareth Village – a delightful recreation of a Galilean Jewish village in the time of Jesus, illustrating the context of Jesus' parables. Our tour includes a threshing floor, olive press, watchtower over fields and vineyards, shepherds, wine press, homes, carpentry, and a life-sized synagogue. Here we will unroll the scrolls and read in memory of Jesus *"The Spirit of the Lord is upon me, because he has anointed me to proclaim good news to the poor. He has sent me to proclaim freedom for the prisoners and recovery of sight for the blind, to set oppressed free, to proclaim the year of the Lord's favor"* (Luke 4:18-19).

Mt Precipice – rejection of Jesus by his hometown.

Dinner & Overnight in Tiberias hotel or a kibbutz guest house along the lakeshore.

Day 4 – Around the Lake: Becoming a Disciple of Jesus

Mt. of Beatitudes – Kingdom of Heaven teaching. Ascend Mt of Beatitudes where we enjoy time for spiritual reflection and meditation on Jesus' teachings from the "Sermon on the Mount" *(Matt 5-7)*.

The Primacy of St. Peter / Tabgha – Communion at the seashore of the lake – Region of the multiplication of loaves & fishes. Jesus feeds his disciples before sending them out.

Capernaum – The Gospels name this fishing town as the headquarters of Jesus' public ministry in Galilee *(Mark 1:31-38, Matt 4:13)*. Capernaum was the home of Peter, the location of many miraculous healings, powerful teachings, and yet a town that Jesus eventually cursed for their unbelief *(Matt 11:23)*. The centurion's faith in Jesus to heal his servant, prompted Jesus to... *(Luke 7:1-10)*.

Tax station along Via Maris – border of political territory Herod Antipas/ Herod Philip. Jesus calls a tax collector to be a disciple – Matthew *(Mark 2:14)*.

Lunch – St Peter's Fish

Boat Ride – enjoy the last moments of Jesus' beloved landscape as we sail around the Sea of Galilee on the "Jesus Boat" – a replica of a wooden fishing boat used by fishermen in the time of Jesus. Then see a real one from the 1st century recently discovered on the lakeshore.

Baptisms at Yardenit – a spiritual highlight for every Christian group, we will celebrate our baptism with full water immersion. This facility is located where the lake feeds into the Jordan River, just before it meanders south through the Jordan Valley.

Migdal – visit the recently discovered 1st century AD synagogue in the hometown of Mary Magdalene. Discuss the role of female disciples in Jesus' ministry and the early church.

Dinner & Overnight in Tiberias hotel or a kibbutz guest house along the lakeshore.

Day 5 – Exploring the Golan: Messiah Declared Amongst the Gentiles

Drive through the Hula Valley, a resting point for millions of birds' annual migration between Europe and Africa. Israel is also a blessed land bridge for God's creatures.

Metula – Drive through Golan to a viewpoint with the Lebanese border.

Tel Dan – the altar of Jeroboam, the northern kingdom of Israel destroyed by the Assyrians. We will enjoy a short hike through the beautiful nature reserve of Dan, and see the ancient gate of Jeroboam, king of northern tribes of Israel, and the remains of the altar he constructed (with golden calf) to replace the Temple worship in Jerusalem. The powerful springs of Dan are the primary source of water for Jordan River, supplying 1/3 of Israel's water.

Lunch Break

Caesarea Philippi – the ancient Roman city of Caesarea Philippi (also called Banias for the worship of Greek demi-god Pan). Here Jesus asked His disciples, "who do men say that I am" *(Mark 8:27-30 and Matt 16:13-20)*. Simon (Peter) declares Jesus to be the Messiah, and Jesus renames him Peter – *"on this rock I will build my church."* The nearby slopes of snowy white Mt Hermon, are the possible location of the magnificent Transfiguration of Jesus. Along this ancient trade route, also recall Saul's dramatic encounter with Jesus on the Road to Damascus.

Har Bental – Viewpoint of the Syrian border

Dinner & Overnight in Tiberias hotel or a kibbutz guest house along the lakeshore.

Day 6 – The Jordan Valley: Jordan River & Dead Sea
Check out from hotel

Beit She'an – Today, you're heading south driving along the Jordan Valley. Your next stop will be the ancient city of Beit She'an. On the walls of this once-powerful city that controlled the gateway to the land of Israel, the Philistines hung the bodies of Saul and his three sons, whom they had defeated in battle on nearby Mount Gilboa. You can climb to the top of the huge mound of biblical antiquities, and see many magnificent remnants of this city that was the capital of the Decapolis cities where the Gospels say the fame of Jesus spread during his public ministry.

Then via the Jordan Valley – we descend through the Syrian-African Great Rift Valley to the lowest point on earth.

Bypass **Jericho** – the most ancient city in the world, this oasis of natural springs and palm trees was first inhabited 9000 years ago. Conquered by resounding trumpets as Joshua led the Israelites around the heavily fortified walls of Jericho. Nearby is the view of the monastery on Mt.

Qarantal (Mount of Temptation) commemorates how the Holy Spirit immediately led Jesus into the wilderness for 40 days of fasting in the face of the temptations of Satan.

Qasr el Yahud – the traditional site where John baptized Jesus in the Jordan River *(Mark 1:9)*. Somewhere near Jericho, Joshua led the Israelite tribes into the Promised Land. God stopped the Jordan River for the priests to safely carry the Ark of the Covenant across to the other side.

Lunch Break

Qumran – Explore the archeology of the Jewish "Essene" sect, which turned away from the Temple worship & sacrifice during the corrupt Hasmonean period. Unique findings are multiple mikveh (ritual purity baths), a scriptorium, and a community dining hall, but no individual homes. In the nearby caves, the famous Dead Sea Scrolls were discovered in 1947. They prove the Hebrew Bible has not been altered in 2200 years. Discuss the possible relationship of the Essenes / Dead Sea Sect to the ministry and preaching of John the Baptist in the same wilderness region.

Dinner & (2) Overnights in the Dead Sea area.

Day 7 – Judean Wilderness: The Desert as a Refuge

Masada – one of Herod the Great's magnificent fortresses and the last Jewish stronghold to fall captive to the Romans. Here we will discuss the nature of the Herodian dynasty and Zealot ideology. On our way back north, we will pass by the beautiful subtropical oasis of En Gedi before making our way to the site of Qumran.

Ein Gedi – Hike the hiding place of King David from King Saul

Dead Sea – Enjoy a swim (or rather a float!) in the mineral-rich waters of the Dead Sea, renowned for its minerals and healing properties.

Dinner & Overnight in the Dead Sea area.

Day 8 – The Northern Negev: Our Patriarchs

Check out from hotel.

Today we will explore the Northern Negev and the lifestyle of our Patriarchs and Matriarchs.

Camel Land Ranch – (**1 hour ride**) Along the northern Incense Route.

Tel Be'er Sheva – Tel Sheva / Tel Be'er Sheva in Hebrew and Tel es-Saba in Arabic is an archeological site in southern Israel believed to be the remains of the biblical town of Be'er Sheva – the area in which Abraham, Isaac, and Jacob lived and worked.

The Elah Valley – The Elah Valley or the Valley of Elah is a long shallow valley in Israel and the West Bank, best known as the place described in the Old Testament where the Israelites were encamped when David fought Goliath.

Continue the Ascent up to Jerusalem.

Dinner and (4) Overnights in Jerusalem.

Day 9 – The Hillcountry of Judea: God Establishes His Kingdom

Mount of Olives' observation deck beholds the breathtaking panorama of the Holy City. Recount the biblical events that took place on Mt Olives and Kidron Valley below. Celebrate Jesus' triumphant entrance to Jerusalem as we walk together down the Palm Sunday Route.

Dominus Flevit church, commemorating where Jesus wept over the future destruction of Jerusalem *(Luke 19:41)*.

Garden of Gethsemane, with its ancient olive grove, and the Church of Agony (modern Church of All Nations). This is where Jesus prayed on the night of his betrayal by Judas and was arrested by Roman soldiers *(Matt. 26:36, John 18:1)*.

Drive across the **Kidron Valley**, also called the Valley of Jehoshaphat – prophesied site of Final Judgement. See all the tombs here, each religious group poised for Resurrection Day.

Mt Zion – House of Caiaphas – Peter's denial of Jesus .

Lunch Break at Mahane Yehuda Jewish Open Market

The Israel Museum – See an impressive Model of Jerusalem before it was destroyed by the Romans and the Shrine of the Book that houses the Dead Sea Scrolls.

Dinner & Overnight in Jerusalem.

Day 10 – Bethlehem: The Birth of Christ

City of David – Hezekiah's Tunnel – Pool of Siloam – Explore the original City of David, a small Jebusite fortified hilltop conquered by King David's men through an underground shaft. We will see evidence of royal quarters here throughout the Biblical periods. Discover the 1st Temple period, the building of Jerusalem as a political & religious center, and King Hezekiah's projects to protect the Holy City from Assyrian invasion. Option to walk through Hezekiah's Water Tunnel. Our journey ends at the Pool of Siloam, where Jesus healed the blind man. It's possible to ascend on the original Herodian steps to the market street of the Temple Complex.

Then we will drive to **Bethlehem** – Birthplace of King David, and later the birthplace of his descendant Jesus – Emmanuel.

Church of Nativity – The oldest church in the world, built by Roman Emperor Constantine's mother Queen Helena in 4th c AD. Witness how Middle Eastern Christians preserve the holy site where Christ was born.

Lunch Break

Shepherds Fields – where the angels announced the birth of Jesus. We will see actual shepherds grazing their sheep on the hillsides of this modern town.

Dinner & Overnight in Jerusalem.

Day 11 – Last Week of Jesus in Jerusalem
An Earlier Start (Modest Dress Required)

The Temple Mount Origin of the holy site. It begins with Mt. Moriah, where Abraham almost sacrificed his son Isaac. Believed to be the same rocky hilltop where King David purchased the threshing floor (2 Samuel 24:18-25), intended to house the Ark of the Covenant. His son King Solomon built the First Temple and royal palaces on this hilltop overlooking the newly established City of David.

Pools of Bethesda – where Jesus healed a paralytic *(John 5:1-15)*. The Crusaders built a magnificent church honoring St Anne, the mother of Mary. The excellent acoustics provide the best place to sing in Jerusalem.

Antonia Fortress (Praetorian), where Jesus stood before Pontius Pilate and was condemned to death by crucifixion *(Mark 15:1)*.

Via Dolorosa – a walk remembering Jesus suffering as he carried the cross to Golgotha / the place of the skull.

Holy Sepulchre Church – Traditional site of Calvary/ Golgotha – the place of Jesus' crucifixion and burial – 4th c AD "Church of the Resurrection."

Discover the historical authenticity of the site, the centuries of religious traditions, and the nature of worship here until today.

Rooftop view to Temple Mount today – 35-acre platform featuring golden Dome of Rock & Al Aqsa Mosque. 3rd most holy site in Islam. Discuss how each religious group through history has revered the Temple Mount area.

Lunch Break

Biblical Archeology in Jewish Quarter – see the "**Broad Wall**" built by King Hezekiah to protect Israelite refugees from Assyrian attack, warnings of the Prophet Isaiah. Destruction of the city 120 years later by Babylonians, then exiled Jews return to Zion with Nehemiah & Ezra. Rebuild walls & the temple and reestablish worship & reading Torah.

Davidson Center – Jesus and all other pilgrims ascend to the Temple in the same manner. We will stand on the actual **Southern Steps** to the Temple Mount, and learn about the requirements of ritual purity, temple tax, and sacrifice. Importance of Herod's Temple to Christians – Jesus would have walked on these steps. He was brought to the Temple several times in childhood – after birth – as a young boy, teaching with authority in his father's house. Jesus and his disciples visited the Temple continuously during his last week in Jerusalem before his arrest. Overturned the moneychanger tables, in an attempt to purify his father's house. Jesus finally prophesied its destruction *(Mark 13:1-2)*. The Southern Steps are also a possible site of Peter's sermon on Pentecost and baptism of 3000 on the festival of Shavuot. See evidence of the magnificent Temple built by King Herod that was destroyed by the Romans 100 years later. Internal struggles and factions within Judaism led to the Great Revolt and final destruction of the Temple in 70 AD.

Western Wall – The holiest site in the world for the Jewish faithful. Closest to where the Holy of Holies once stood. This wall is actually just a portion of the retaining wall of Herod's Temple mount platform, the only remains of the Temple after destruction by the Romans in 70 AD.

End the day at the **Garden Tomb** – we will have a special time of prayer, worship, and communion.

Dinner & Overnight in Jerusalem

Day 12 – Depends on Flights Departure Time

Check out from hotel and identify luggage.

Return home with cheerful memories of the land.

Itinerary – subject to change according to flight arrival & departure times, inclement weather, security concerns, and the wishes of the group.

Maps

[#1] Geographical Regions

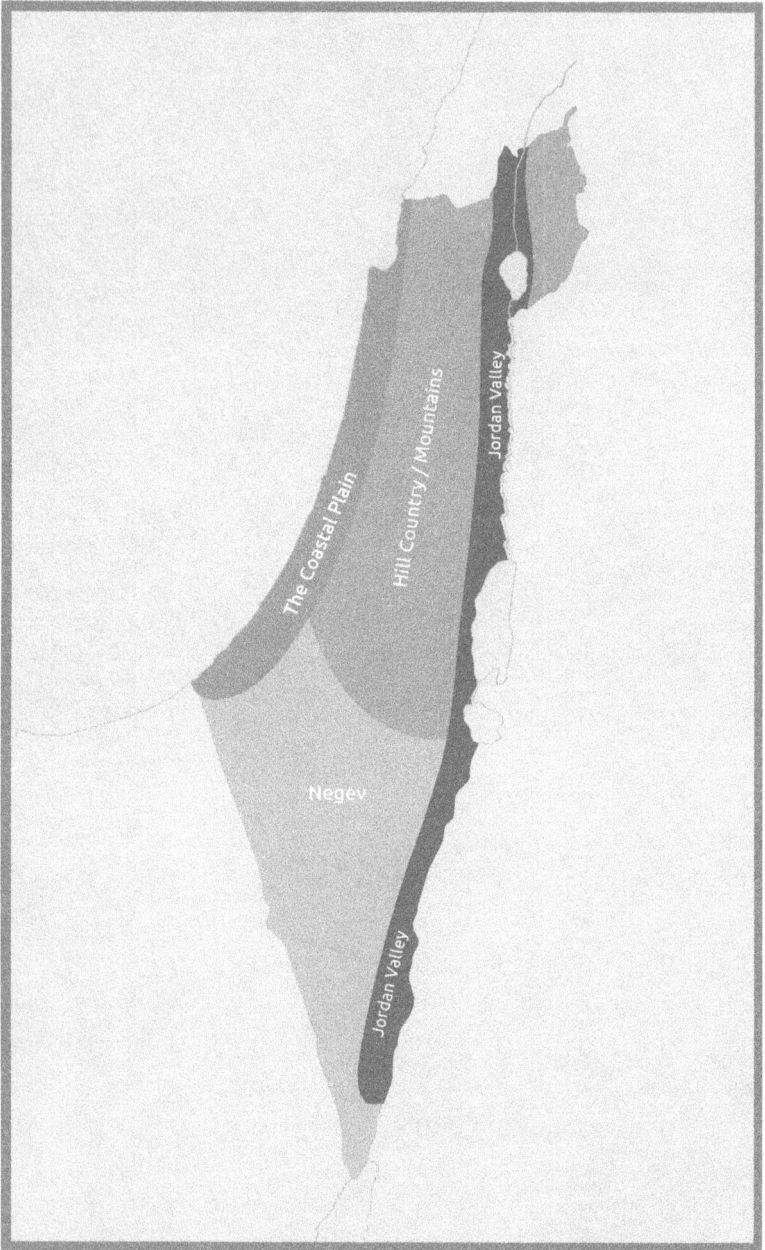

[#2] Israel & Neighbors

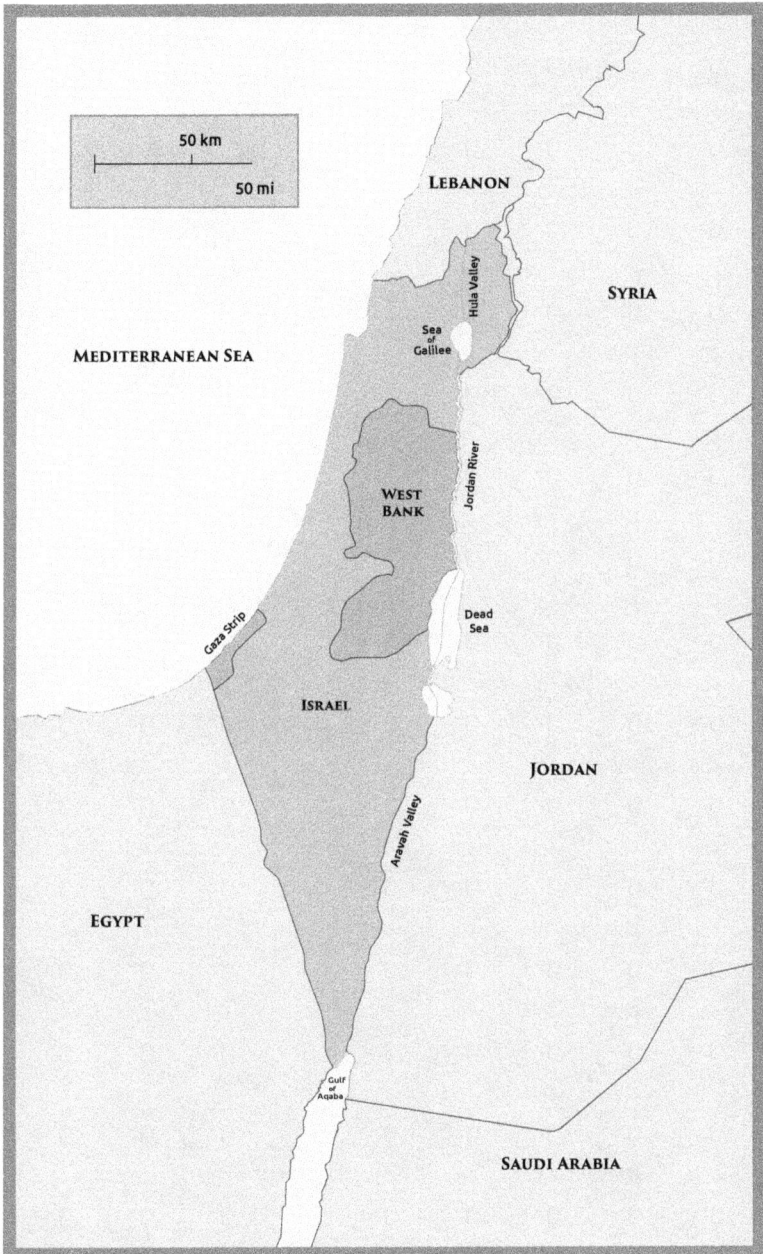

[#3] Israel Sites

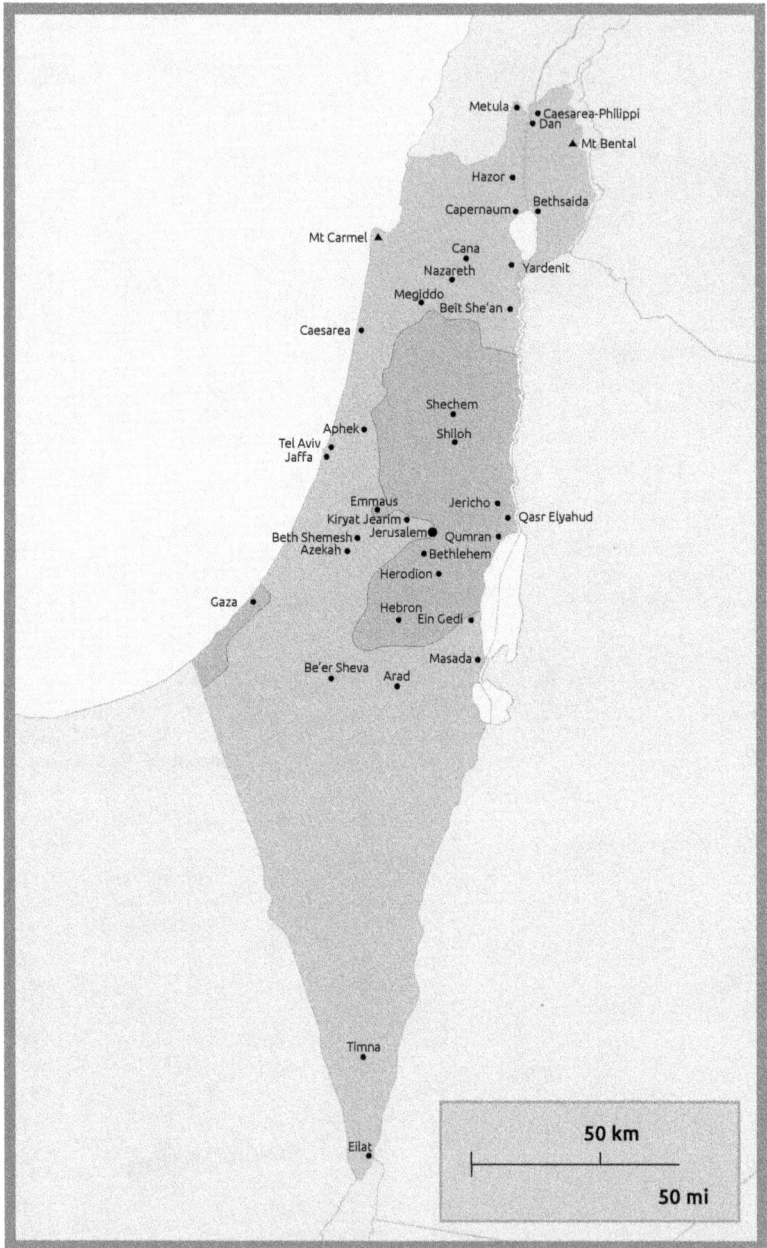

[#4] Sea of Galilee Sites

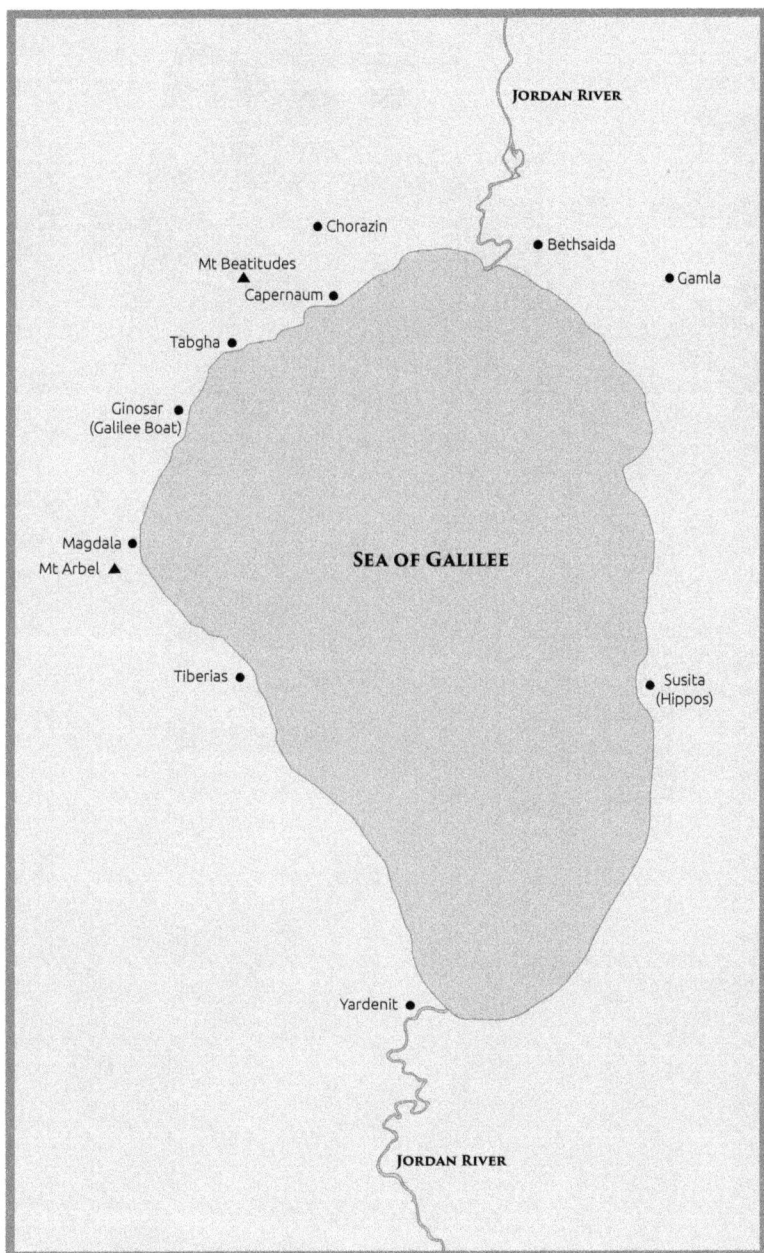

[#5] Old City Jerusalem Today

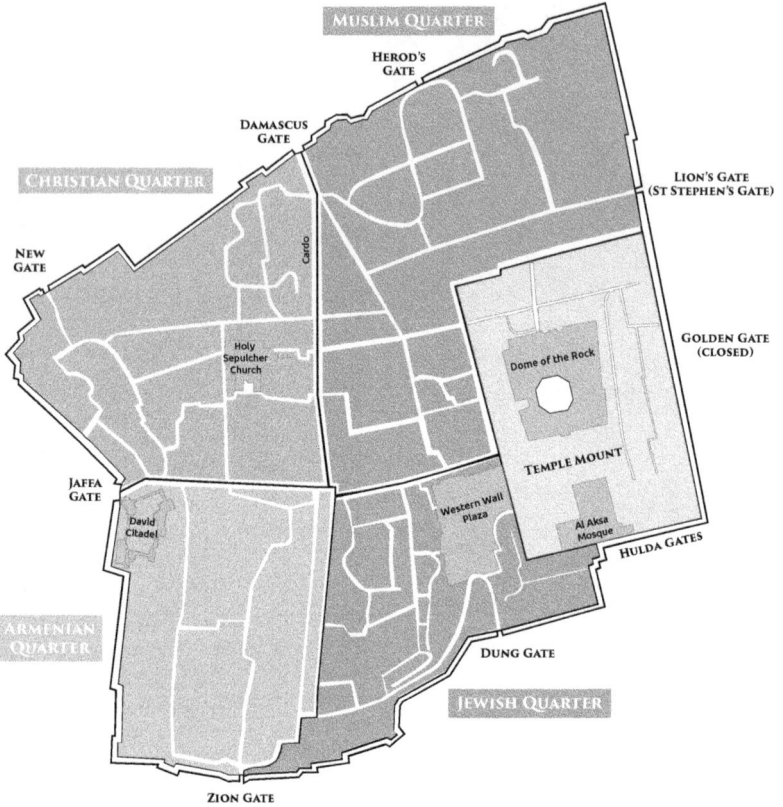

MUSLIM QUARTER

HEROD'S GATE

DAMASCUS GATE

CHRISTIAN QUARTER

LION'S GATE
(ST STEPHEN'S GATE)

NEW GATE

Cardo

Holy Sepulcher Church

GOLDEN GATE
(CLOSED)

Dome of the Rock

TEMPLE MOUNT

JAFFA GATE

David Citadel

Western Wall Plaza

Al Aksa Mosque

HULDA GATES

ARMENIAN QUARTER

DUNG GATE

JEWISH QUARTER

ZION GATE

[#6] The West Bank

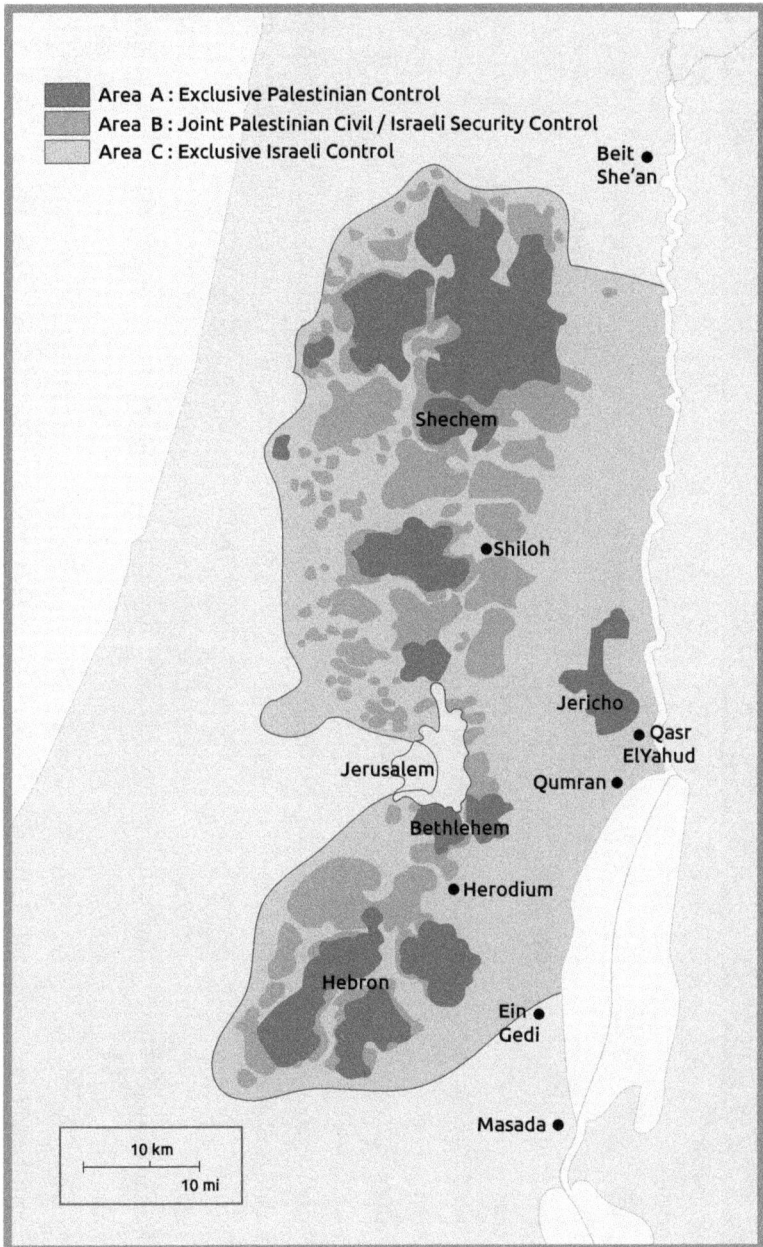

Area A : Exclusive Palestinian Control
Area B : Joint Palestinian Civil / Israeli Security Control
Area C : Exclusive Israeli Control

Beit ●
She'an

Shechem

●Shiloh

Jericho
● Qasr
ElYahud
Qumran ●

Jerusalem

Bethlehem

●Herodium

Hebron

Ein ●
Gedi

Masada ●

10 km
10 mi

Distances

From - Km /(Miles)	Eilat	Be'er Sheva	Tiberias	Haifa	Tel Aviv	Jerusalem
Jerusalem	309 (193)	81 (50)	152 (95)	151 (94)	58 (36)	-
Tel Aviv	346 (220)	105 (65)	134 (83)	95 (59)	-	58 (36)
Haifa	438 (273)	197 (123)	69 (43)	-	95 (59)	151 (94)
Tiberias	405 (253)	233 (145)	-	69 (43)	134 (83)	152 (95)
Beer Sheba	241 (150)	-	233 (145)	197 (123)	105 (65)	81 (50)
Eilat	-	241 (150)	405 (253)	438 (273)	346 (120)	309 (193)
Ben-Gurion Airport	354 (221)	113 (70)	133 (83)	107 (66)	15 (9)	43 (26)
Arad	219 (136)	45 (28)	234 (146)	242 (151)	150 (93)	100 (62)
Ashkelon	307 (190)	66 (41)	183 (114)	157 (98)	54 (33)	71 (44)
Beit Shean	368 (230)	195 (121)	37 (23)	70 (43)	117 (73)	115 (71)
Beit Shemesh	333 (208)	92 (57)	169 (105)	136 (85)	42 (26)	27 (16)
Banias (Golan)	475 (296)	303 (189)	70 (43)	114 (71)	204 (127)	222 (138)
Jericho	289 (180)	163 (101)	116 (72)	149 (93)	97 (60)	36 (22)
Metula	469 (293)	297 (185)	64 (40)	120 (75)	198 (123)	216 (135)
Mitzpe Ramon	148 (92)	80 (50)	313 (195)	277 (173)	185 (115)	161 (100)
Nazareth	488 (305)	207 (129)	29 (18)	35 (21)	102 (63)	131 (81)
Netanya	372 (232)	131 (81)	101(63)	66 (41)	29 (18)	85 (53)
Sdom (Dead Sea)	195 (121)	79 (49)	210 (131)	275 (171)	184 (115)	124 (77)

III. Navigating the Logistics of Complicated Sites

CHAPTER NINE

TLV – Tel Aviv "Ben Gurion" Airport Arrivals Procedures

Before Arrival:
If you missed your connecting flight, contact us immediately and send us your new flights details with the exact arrival time to Israel.
E-mail: info@twinstours.com

Upon Arrival:
Follow the signs (and the crowds) to Passport Control.

At Passport Control:
Keep together as a group. As the Group Leader, you should be the first person to speak to the passport control agent. Explain you are on a tour of biblical sites. Have the tour itinerary / list of hotels on Twins Tours letterhead ready in case you need to show them to the agent.

Answer questions honestly, without giving more information than you are asked. Don't ramble or joke, and don't get anxious or angry. You are a tourist coming to learn more about the Bible and Israel. **Warning**: Don't mention anything about "Missions," "Outreach," or "Evangelism."

Everyone's passport will be examined. If someone's passport has stamps form an Arab/Muslim country, or if they have an Arabic/Muslim-sounding name, they may be taken aside for further questioning. If this happens, stay calm, cooperate and notify Twins Tours (there is free Wi-Fi, see details above). Designate someone responsible to stay with the person being questioned, their spouse/relative/friend, while you take the rest of the group into Baggage Claim.

Everyone will receive a Tourist Entry Visa (a blue slip of paper) that they must keep with their passport at all times until their departure from Israel. (Israel no longer stamps passports, so don't worry about jeopardizing any future travels.) Everyone must scan their entry visa at the electronic gates situated just before the Baggage Claim. Airport staff will be nearby to help with the scanning process.

At this time, each person should put their passport (with the blue slip of paper / Tourist Entry Visa) in a secure place, so the passport does not get lost during the baggage claim procedure. We suggest placing them in the name tag holder.

At Baggage Claim:

The luggage trolleys in arrivals cost 10 shekels, you can use your credit card to rent the trolleys.

Report any missing luggage to the Missing Baggage counter. Give the name and city of your first hotel as the address to which the bags should be delivered, and give them the Tour guide number or our office number. All these details should already be supplied by the Twins Tours Team in Israel before your travels. **You will receive a reference number. Do not leave without it, otherwise you will not get your luggage back.** Give this paperwork to the Twins Tours representative meeting you in the Arrivals Hall so we can help follow-up and locate any missing luggage.

Exit the Baggage Claim area as a group. Once you leave this area, it is forbidden to return, so make sure nothing is left behind. For security reasons, do not leave any bags unattended anywhere in the airport.

Arrivals Hall:

Head towards the Right-side Exit, and look for a person holding a sign with your name (or your tour group/church's name) written on it. If you don't see the sign, gather the group together near the chairs, and wait for the Twins Tours representative to find you. If necessary, contact us using the free airport Wi-Fi.

Meeting the Tour Guide:

Once you have located the tour guide, he will introduce himself and check:

- That the group is all together.
- That everyone has all their luggage.
- If anyone needs to use the bathroom. Remember, there could be a long drive ahead, and there are no toilet facilities on the bus.

Changing Money:

There is no need for everyone to change money immediately (you will get better rates elsewhere). If you need shekels to start you off, there is a money exchange counter in the Baggage Claim area and another in the Arrivals Hall. Take care of the money changing while the group is having a final toilet break before departure.

Boarding the Tour Bus:

Follow the guide, as a group, to the bus. The driver will help put large pieces of luggage in the luggage compartment. People should take all small or personal items on board with them.

Once everyone is seated, do a headcount and double-check that everyone has their passports before you leave the airport. The first row of seats is reserved for you and the tour guide. If someone gets motion sickness, they should sit in the second row.

The tour guide will introduce himself and the driver. The guide will distribute maps of Israel and give other information from the Twins Tours Office. He will also distribute one free bottle of water to everyone on the first day – it helps with getting over the jet lag. During the trip, water can always be bought from the driver for $1 a bottle.

The guide will then invite you to speak on the microphone to the group, to say a prayer, or just some words of guidance as the journey begins.

Once you are on the road, enjoy the start of the journey of your once in a lifetime experience.

CHAPTER TEN

Israeli Hotel Customs and Information

While Israeli hotels are mostly the same as hotels all over the world, there are a few areas where adherence to Jewish law and customs makes them unique, notably, in adherence to the Sabbath and keeping kosher (Jewish dietary restrictions).

Experiencing Shabbat in a Hotel

The 25 hours, from an hour before sundown on Friday night to sundown on Saturday, are known as Shabbat, the Jewish Sabbath. You'll notice over this period that things are run slightly differently in your hotel than during the week:

- Candles are traditionally lit to mark the start of the Sabbath. To – safely – allow this ritual to take place, there will be trays of candles and matches in the lobby or near the dining room. Women and girls will light two candles, cover their eyes and say the following blessing: "Blessed are You, Lord our God, King of the universe, who has sanctified us with His commandments, and commanded us to kindle the light of the holy Shabbat." If any of the women in the group want to participate in this experience, they should feel free to do so – no one is checking to see who is lighting. If they want to say a prayer, they should do so quietly to themselves. The candles are lit prior to sundown (40 minutes before sundown in Jerusalem and 18 minutes in all other places).

- Most hotels will have prayers taking place on Friday night and Saturday morning, either in the hotel synagogue if there is one, or in a room designated as a synagogue for the duration of the Sabbath.

- Once the prayer service is over, the eating begins! Food plays a major part in the Sabbath (and in much of Jewish life). The Friday night meal will be bigger and more extravagant than other meals, so enjoy the extra food, but remember you might have to wait for a free table and fight your way through the crowds to the food. The lobby area will also be busier and noisier than on other days as families relax together.

- During the meal, you will see and hear people making a blessing over wine/grape juice, which is the customary way to start a Shabbat meal. They say: Blessed are You, God, Ruler of the universe, who creates the fruit of the vine.

- You will also see diners making a blessing over two plaited loaves/buns, called **Challot** (A Challah, is a special and delicious type of bread only for Shabbat). Without this blessing (Blessed are You, Lord our God, King of the universe, who has brought forth bread from the earth) no matter how much food is served and eaten, the meal is not considered ritually complete.

- Before they make the blessing over the bread, Jewish diners will wash their hands at wash stations situated around the dining room. This is a spiritual/ritual cleansing that takes place before eating bread. Anyone who wants to experience this is free to do so.

- Before, during, and after the meal, people will be singing. The Friday night meal begins with a couple of hymns, including "A Woman of Valor" (Proverbs 31:10), and ends with the Grace After Meals. During the meal, you may also hear singing since it is customary to sing joyful and happy songs on the Sabbath.

- Because electricity cannot be used over the Sabbath, much of the food (especially on Saturday) will have been prepared in advance and reheated on hotplates. There will not be fresh items such as omelets or pancakes. The coffee machines will be covered up, and only regular coffee will be available on a Saturday morning in the dining room and in the lobby/hotel coffee shop. If you love coffee, we recommend bringing your favorite coffee like starbucks via packets with you (and you can bring some for me too).

- To avoid Jewish guests using electricity, the hotel will run a Shabbat elevator throughout the Sabbath. This is a regular elevator programmed to run automatically, without having to press any buttons. It will stop at each floor for a short time and buzz before the door closes, giving everyone enough time to get in and out. There will usually still be other lifts running as normal. If there is only a Shabbat elevator, give yourself extra time to get up and down.

- Things will probably take longer on the Sabbath than during the rest of the week. Although Jews are not supposed to work on the Sabbath, there will still be many Jewish members of staff visible in the hotel on Friday night and Saturday, since many choose not to adhere to these religious laws. However, you might notice more staff who are Arab, Russian, or even foreign workers who are not Jewish and do not need to follow these dictates.

- Friday night check-in may be busier than usual and take longer than during the rest of the week since many locals may also be checking in for the weekend.

- Saturday night check-in may be more complicated than usual, since many hotels offer guests late checkout to ensure the rules of the Sabbath are not violated. This means a Saturday night check-in can be quite late – up to three hours past sundown. However, you will still be able to eat dinner at the normal time in the dining room, and the hotel will provide a conference room, allowing you to hold an evening meeting until the rooms are available for check-in.

- If you want to use a meeting room for your group during Shabbat, be aware there will be some limitations and you will not be able to use microphones, speakers, or projectors.

The Dining Room

- Since almost all hotels in Israel operate kosher kitchens and dining rooms, only kosher meat and fish will be served. This means, primarily, chicken, turkey, or beef that has been killed in a ritually acceptable way and fish that have both fins and scales. Kosher hotels will never serve bacon, pork, or shellfish.

- Due to the strictures against serving a calf in its mother's milk (Exodus 23:19 and 34:26 and Deuteronomy 14:21), kosher restaurants in hotels and elsewhere will not serve dairy and meat products at the same meal. This means that you will not be able to have butter on your bread at dinner, and you will never find sausages served at breakfast.

- In hotels with kosher dining halls, breakfast will always be a dairy meal (with plenty of cheese products) and dinner will always be a meat meal (with many different meat/poultry items).

- At both breakfast and dinner, fish and eggs will be served. These products are considered to be pareve, that is, they are neither meat nor dairy and can be eaten freely alongside both cheese and chicken (or any other kosher meat).

- Make sure you don't bring in outside food (even ice cream) into the Lobby Coffee Bar or Restaurant, since it might not be kosher.

Other Things You Might Notice

- Because religious Jewish couples observe a period of intimate separation each month (with a basis in Leviticus 15:19), Israeli hotels don't usually offer double or king sized beds. Instead, there are "double" beds made up of two single beds pushed together and fitted with one large sheet.

- Wherever you go in Israel, you will see two-handled pitchers in many bathrooms. These are for people to use for ritual washing after using the bathroom or before eating bread. They can be made from all sorts of material including plastic, metal or even pottery.

- Above all, don't worry about making mistakes and don't be embarrassed to ask if something doesn't make sense. Hotel staff are used to guests who aren't Jewish and will be more than happy to explain things to you or answer any questions.

CHAPTER ELEVEN

The National Parks

There are over forty **National Parks** in Israel ranging from archaeological sites such as Caesarea National Park and Masada to sites of natural beauty such as the Carmel National Park. There are so many parks to choose from to visit.

The itineraries that Twins Tours develop, such as the one you read in the earlier pages of this book, include the most important national parks related to Christianity.

List of Sites under National Parks Authority

Nimrod Fortress	Bar'am
Hermon Stream (Banias)	Amud Stream
Tel Dan	Korazim
Senir Stream	Betiha (Magrase)
Horshat Tal	Yehudiya
Iyon stream	Gamla
Hula	Arbel
Tel Hazor	Kursi (Gerassa)
Akhziv	Hamat Tiberias
Yehi'am Fortress	Kokhav Hayarden (Belvoir)

Ma'ayan Harod	The Monastery of St. Martyrius
Bet Alpha	The Monastery of St. Euthymius
Gan Hashelosha (Sahne)	En Prat
Bet She'an	Herodium
Zippori	Mount Gerizim
Bet She'arim	Qumran
Hai-Bar Carmel	Enot Tsukim
Nahal Me'arot	En Gedi
Taninim Stream	En Gedi Antiquities
Dor Habonim Beach	Masada
En Afek	Tel Arad
Tel Megiddo (Armageddon)	Tel Be'er Sheva
Caesarea	Besor (Eshkol)
Apollonia	Mamshit
Yarkon-Afek	En Avdat
Tel Ashkelon	Avdat
Bet Guvrin (Maresha)	Makhtesh Ramon Visitors Center
Stalactite Cave	/ Bio Ramon
En Hemed	Hai-Bar Yotvata
Castel	Eilat Coral Beach
The Inn of the Good Samaritan	

** The cable car at Masada is not included

** City of David is not included

Most sites are open 8:00-17:00 in Summer and 8:00-16:00 in Winter. Fridays and Holiday eves 8:00-15:00 in Summer and 8:00-14:00 in Winter.

Last entrance to the site is one hour before closing time.

CHAPTER TWELVE

The Dead Sea

The Dead Sea is situated between the hills of Judaea to the west and the Transjordanian plateaus to the east. Before the water level began dropping, the lake was some 50 miles (80 km) long, attained a maximum width of 11 miles (18 km), and had a surface area of about 394 square miles (1,020 square km).

The peninsula of Al-Lisān "The Tongue" (the shape of this peninsula looks like a tongue) divides the lake on its eastern side into two unequal basins: the northern basin encompassed about three-fourths of the lake's total surface area and reached a depth of 1,300 feet (400 metres), and the southern basin was smaller and considerably shallower, less than 10 feet (3 metres) deep on average. All the resort hotels are located in the southern part of the dead sea, the area is called by the name "Ein Bokek."

During biblical times and until the 8th century BC, only the area around the northern basin was inhabited, and the lake was slightly lower than its present-day level. It rose to its highest level, 1,275 feet (389 meters) below sea level, in 1896 but receded again after 1935, stabilizing at about 1,300 feet (400 meters) below sea level for several decades.

The Dead Sea, also known as the Salt Sea, is the lowest location on earth. This lake is also one of the saltiest bodies of water in the world. With 34% salinity (8 times as salty as the ocean), its density allows for a relaxing float because of natural buoyancy.

One of the highlights of a trip to Israel is taking a dip (or rather, a float) in the mineral-rich waters of the Dead Sea and enjoying the healing properties of its detoxifying black mud.

That being said, there are a few **precautions** and things to keep in mind as you and your team visit this incredible place:

- The Dead Sea is **NOT** for diving and swimming.

- Do Not put your face underwater.

- Do Not open eyes underwater (or rub one's eye with wet hands).

- Do not shave the night before (preferable two days before).

- If there is a cut, the salt burns – it's healing, but it's okay to get out.

- Be aware that children are more sensitive to high salinity.

- Do not go to Jordan please stay in Israel.

Entering the Dead Sea

- Take small steps when entering as there are holes. Then sit down slowly and lean back. Like a crab, you will naturally float!

- The best mud is a couple of meters off the shoreline inside the water. The mud there is less likely to have stones.

- Your skin will feel very oily from the salt and minerals.

- It is not recommended to stay for more than 30 minutes in the water.

What to Bring

- Sunscreen!! (We are in the desert).

- Water shoes.

- Swim suit.

- Bag – with a towel, change of clothes, washing soap, etc. (it is required to change before going back on the bus).

- Bottle of water (to drink, and to wash eyes if they get wet).

- Keep an eye out on your phone (Recommended to keep unnecessary belongings on the bus).

- Do not go into the water with jewelry and especially rings.

Dead sea facts you didn't know

Almost everyone knows that The Dead Sea, a salt lake shared between Israel and Jordan, is one of the world's most unique sites in the world, but did you know these interesting facts about it?

1. *Why is it salty?*
   The Dead Sea's salinity is 34.2% (compared with the Mediterranean's 3.5%). It is the fourth saltiest body of water in the world, ranking behind Antarctica's Don Juan Pond and Lake Vanda, and Djibouti's Lake Assal. One of the reasons for the high salinity is that the Dead Sea doesn't pour out. Additionally, the arid desert climate causes evaporation, increasing salinity.

2. *Is it possible to drown in it?*
   Although whoever enters the water immediately floats, you should keep in mind that it is still possible to drown in the Dead Sea. This happens when swimmers get caught in strong winds, flip over

and swallowing the salty water. Always make sure to only enter proclaimed beaches, in the presence of a lifeguard.

3. *Can you dive in it?*

    Believe it or not, you can also dive in the Dead Sea! It takes unique diving skills, and those who possess them will enjoy spectacular geological salt formations.

4. *Why is it called The Dead Sea?*

    The high salinity means that no life can evolve in the Dead Sea, which gave it the moniker "Sea of Death". But are there absolutely zero life forms in the Dead Sea? Not exactly. Some bacteria and fungus can survive in these waters.

5. *Why is it so popular?*

    The Dead Sea is a popular tourist destination for many reasons, one of which is its medicinal values. The water of the Dead Sea contains 26 beneficial minerals, and the air contains minimal amounts of dust and allergens compared to other places in the world. Apart from dipping in the sea and in sulfur-rich pools in the surrounding spa resorts, many rub themselves with the black mud found at its banks, which is said to relieve different skin issues. The Dead Sea may be the biggest free spa on earth.

CHAPTER THIRTEEN

The Sea of Galilee

The Sea of Galilee is located in northeastern Israel, near the borders with Jordan and Syria.

It is not really a sea, it is a freshwater lake and it is not really a big lake either, it is only 53 kilometers (33 miles) in circumference, about 21 kilometers (13 miles) long, and 13 kilometers (8.1 miles) wide. The Sea of Galilee's maximum depth is roughly 43 meters (141 feet).

The Sea of Galilee is the lowest freshwater lake on Earth The Sea is known by many names and is referred to by Israelis as the "Kinneret," which is Hebrew for "harp" considered to be the shape resembling the lake.

Facts about the Sea of Galilee

1. It is Israel's largest source of fresh drinking water, supplying about one-third of the nation's annual water requirement.

2. The Sea is believed to be where Jesus walked on water, calmed the storm, and preached from a fishing boat.

3. Its closest major city is Tiberias, which is considered one of Israel's holy cities.The Talmud holy scriptures are believed to have been written in Tiberias.

The Boat Ride & Boat Museum

Yes, it is as amazing an experience as it sounds!

There are several different companies that provide boat rides, all similar in features. Differences may depend on booking availability and group sizes. (please note that larger boats have a minimum requirement for the number of passengers.) The ride includes peaceful worship times, dancing, fishing demonstrations and more!

The Jesus Boat – Another exciting experience is visiting an ancient 2000 year old fishing boat found along the shores of the Galilee in 1986. (Keep in mind it requires an additional small fee).

History of Jesus Boat Museum

In 1986, an ancient boat was pulled from the mud along the northwestern shore of the Sea of Galilee. It was a unique and exciting find that gives us an idea of the sort of boat used during the time of Jesus.

The boat appeared due to a great drought during which the waters of the lake receded and was discovered by the brothers Moshe and Yuval Lufan, second-generation fishermen from Kibbutz Ginosar. The brothers reported that when they found the boat, a double rainbow appeared in the sky.

The subsequent archaeological dig was undertaken by members of the Kibbutz Ginosar, the Antiquities Authority, and many volunteers. Pulling the boat from the mud without damaging it — yet quickly enough to extract it before the water rose again — was a delicate process, lasting 12 days and nights. The boat then had to be submerged in a chemical bath for 7 years before it could be displayed.

The boat has been dated to the 1st century AD based on pottery and nails found in association with the boat, radiocarbon dating, and hull construction techniques. Evidence of repeated repairs indicates the boat was used for several decades, perhaps nearly a century. When it was considered beyond repair, all useful wooden parts were removed and the remaining hull sunk to the bottom of the lake.

The Galilee Boat is apparently the type of boat that was used on the Sea of Galilee for both fishing and transportation across the lake. It is likely that this sort of boat was used by Jesus and his disciples, many of whom were fishermen. Boats played a large role in Jesus' life and ministry — they are mentioned 50 times in the Gospels!

There is no evidence connecting the boat to Jesus or his disciples, but it is certainly tantalizing to think that Jesus may have seen the boat sail by out on the Sea of Galilee — or even used it himself. But regardless of its history, the "Jesus boat" is a fascinating artifact that brings to life many of the Gospel accounts.

The Galilee Boat is attractively displayed with informative signs in English. The boat is made of 12 different types of wood and measures 25.5 ft. (8.2 m) long, 7.5 ft. (2.3 m) wide, and 4.1 ft (1.25 m) high. It would have had a crew of five (four rowers and a helmsman) and could carry about 15 additional persons. This seems like a lot for such a humble boat, but men were smaller 2,000 years ago — about 5'5" and 140 pounds.

There is also a souvenir shop inside the museum that we recommend to have a lot of Judaica stuff. Judaica are the objects needed to fulfill God's Torah commandments and to uphold the traditions of the Judaic faith. The commandment to wear the fringe (Numbers 15:37-40) requires a prayer shawl, the commandment to inscribe God's Law on the doorposts (Deuteronomy 6:9) requires a mezuzah. Judaica gives you the chance to not just fulfill, but personalize the commandment and invest yourself in learning more about Jewish traditions.

CHAPTER FOURTEEN

Baptism Sites

There are two baptism sites in Israel.

1. Qasr Elyahud

The traditional site of the Baptism of Jesus is located in the Judean Desert, close to the Dead Sea, and a few meters from the Jordanian baptism site across the river.

Christian tradition marks this site as the place of the "spiritual birth" of Jesus, as opposed to his physical birth in Bethlehem. As such, the baptismal site is of great sacred significance – the third holiest site in the Christian world (after the Church of the Nativity in Bethlehem and the Church of the Holy Sepulchre in Jerusalem).

According to various traditions, the site is also believed to be the place where the Children of Israel crossed the Jordan River and entered the Holy Land after their 40 years of wandering in the desert. It is here that: "as soon as the priests who carry the ark of the Lord—the Lord of all the earth—set foot in the Jordan, its waters flowing downstream will be cut off and stand up in a heap." (Josh 3:13).

Another event attributed to this site is Elijah's ascension to heaven in a fiery chariot after he and Elisha crossed the Jordan: "Elijah took his cloak, rolled it up and struck the water with it. The water divided to the right and to the left, and the two of them crossed over on dry ground." (2 Kings 2:8).

Until 1967 this site, under Jordanian control, saw visits by masses of tourists and pilgrims. In 1968 access to the site was prohibited because of its location beyond the border fence in a closed military zone. Yardenit, south of the Sea of Galilee, was subsequently created as an alternative site for baptism.

2.   Yardenit

This is not the site where Jesus was baptised but the more popular of the two for baptism. It is located where the Jordan River exits the Sea of Galilee and therefore the water is clearer.

Yardenit is under the supervision of the Israeli Health Ministry and is suitable for baptizing all year round, although the recommended time is May to October as the weather is warmer. This is the more popular site for baptism.

Whether you want to get baptized for the first time or for renewal of dedication, the Jordan River baptism is one of the spiritual highlights of the trip!

The Pastor of the group will perform the ceremony accompanied by testimonies, stories, and worship. If there is no pastor, yet the group wants to get baptized, this can be pre-organized as well.

–   The water is under the supervision of the Israeli Health Ministry and is suitable for baptizing all year round, although recommended time is May to October as weather is warmer.

- The sites offer towels and robes for rent or purchase. There are also more special robes available for buying.

- The white robes are required for getting baptized.

- Underclothes / Swimsuits are required as the robes become see-through when wet.

- There are tickets for the showers and dressing rooms available with the baptism kit – please bring shower necessities.

Be aware that there are tiny fish in the river that may nibble at the feet. They are not dangerous. If tourists are uncomfortable, they can move their feet a bit, and the fish will keep a distance.

CHAPTER FIFTEEN

The West Bank & Palestinian Territories

The West Bank and Gaza Strip had been ruled by Jordan and Egypt, respectively, since the 1948 war until 1967. Israel occupied the West Bank and the Gaza Strip in the Six-Day War of 1967 and has since maintained control. In 1980, Israel officially absorbed East Jerusalem and proclaimed the whole of Jerusalem to be its capital.

The term "Palestinian territories" has been used for many years to describe the territories occupied by Israel since 1967, namely the West Bank (including East Jerusalem) and the Gaza Strip.

The term "West Bank" refers to the landlocked territory west of the Jordan River. It is bordered by Jordan to the east and the Green Line separating it and Israel to the north, west, and south. The West Bank is not its own country but has varying levels of Palestinian autonomy throughout the region. *(Refer to Map #6 to get a general idea).*

Area A – Exclusive Palestinian Control
Area B – Joint Palestinian Civil / Israeli Security Control
Area C – Exclusive Israeli Control

As you can see on the map, the West Bank is home to several amazing touristic sites. Qumran, Jericho, and Bethlehem, to name a few. Being local Christians, we have the privilege of guiding in the Palestinian Territories as well as in Israel.

That being said, on days we will be traveling through the area, be aware that we will be crossing several checkpoints. It is therefore imperative for everyone to have their passports with them on those days. The Tour Guide will also let all the group members know at least a day in advance when they will need their passports.

CHAPTER SIXTEEN

Jordan Border Crossing

If you desire to spend a few days in Jordan as part of your Holy Land experience, please allow for a minimum of 2 days in Jordan as driving distance to Petra takes time, and you do not want to miss it.

As Israel and Jordan are at peaceful terms, it is relatively straightforward and easy to enter Jordan through one of three border crossings.

Yitzhak Rabin / Wadi Arava crossing – located south of Israel near Eilat and closer to Petra.

Allenby / King Hussein crossing – this airport-style security terminal is located near Jerusalem and close to the Jordanian capital city of Amman.

Jordan River / Sheikh Hussein crossing – is located north of Israel near the city of Beit She'an.

- **Do not forget your passports!** You are about to enter into a new country.

- Visas are required and will be arranged through Twins Tours.

- There are exit tax fees to enter into Jordan (and back into Israel afterwards if desired) (prices change depending on which border is taken).

- The lines are generally long; please allow enough time at the border crossing for security check.

- Please note that it is forbidden to bring in any Jewish religious objects (yes, even souvenirs) into Jordan as the items may be confiscated.

- Facilities at the borders include currency exchange and VAT refund.

- Once in Jordan, there is the option of returning home from the local airports. Crossing back into Israel and departing from there is also possible if desired.

- Time at the border can take anywhere between 1 hour to 4 hours.

- Please note: your Israeli Tour Guide will not be your tour guide in Jordan. Twins Tours is associated with tour companies in Jordan. And they provide Jordanian guides to give you a local fascinating tour. Your guide will meet you at the Duty Free on the other end of the border. Both guides will stay in contact until you are safe across and on the bus.

IV. Navigating the Logistics of Complicated Sites in Jerusalem

CHAPTER SEVENTEEN

The Old City of Jerusalem

The Old City today is surrounded by 16th-century Ottoman walls, and inside are stories of over 3000 years of history.

Home to the Wailing Wall, the Dome of the Rock, the Holy Sepulchre, and more, the Old City of Jerusalem is the most intense place in the world! This one square kilometer happens to be the heart of Christianity, Judaism, and Islam.

The Old City is accessible by seven gates and divided into four regions called Quarters – the Jewish Quarter, Christian Quarter, Muslim Quarter, and Armenian Quarter – each of them unique in culture, atmosphere, and history.

The *Jewish Quarter*, for example, sees many tourists for its rich connection to archeology and history. The *Christian Quarter* is home to about forty holy sites for Christians and alive with pilgrims. The *Muslim Quarter* has bustling activity due to the famous Shuk – the market gives the impression of an ancient shopping mall. The smallest is the quiet and beautiful corner of the *Armenian Quarter*; this city within a city is home to about 2,500 Armenians who have resided here since antiquity.

Despite the extreme diversity, the locals in this small space learned to coexist in harmony over the years.

The lively markets of the Old City are teeming with beautiful souvenirs. But unless this is a specially designated time for shopping, make sure people do not stop to buy things. They can take a picture or keep in mind which shop interested them for later.

Stay as one group. It is advisable to designate a person to be the last, preferably someone who is tall and can see the guide at the front. The crowdedness of this small space makes it easy for one to get lost, and navigating the Old City is complicated. In the case that someone does indeed get separated from the group and gets lost, communicate in advance that they can ask for directions to go to Jaffa Gate (the main tourist entrance). From there, they can wait for the group. If too much time passed, they could take a taxi to the hotel (again, communicate schedule in advance).

There are bathrooms in different locations around the Old City but are not easy to find, so ask your guide. Usually, tour guides will have more than five stops each day for toilets. Make sure to use the toilets of the hotel every morning before you leave to the bus.

The ancient stones of the Old City have been tread upon for centuries. While that is amazing, it also means that some stones are more worn out than others and can be very slippery. It is imperative, therefore, to have proper footwear. For ladies, avoid wearing heels and especially in rainy seasons.

The Old City has high tourist activity, but be aware that we are entering through quarters of the locals, and there is cross-cultural information to be aware of. When in the Old City, we will likely visit holy sites; therefore, modest dress is required to enter the sites.

When time is given for shopping, a meeting place will be appointed, and general directions and even recommendations may be given. The Old City shops accept both dollars and shekels.

CHAPTER EIGHTEEN

Via Dolorosa

One of the very popular walks to take from Gethsemane to the
Holy Sepulchre starts at Lion's Gate and passes through the Muslim
Quarter on a path the Via Dolorosa ("The Way of Sorrow"). The Via
Dolorosa follows the traditional path Jesus may have walked from
the Antonia fortress – where he was condemned – and to Calvary
– where he was crucified. This Roman Catholic tradition follows 14
stations that are marked along the path. Some stops are Biblical,
while others formed from traditions.

- *First Station*: Jesus is condemned to death (outside the Antonia
  Fortress – today al-Omariya school).
- *Second Station*: Jesus takes up the cross after the flagellation and
  coronation of thorns.
- *Third Station*: Jesus falls the first time under the weight of the
  cross.
- *Fourth Station*: Jesus sees his mother Mary.
- *Fifth Station*: Simon of Cyrene is ordered to carry the cross of
  Jesus.
- *Sixth Station*: St Veronica wipes the blood from Jesus' face and an
  impression of his face remains on the handkerchief.

- *Seventh Station*: Jesus falls for the second time.
- *Eighth Station*: Jesus consoles the Daughters of Jerusalem.
- *Ninth Station*: Jesus falls for the third time.
- *Tenth Station*: Jesus is stripped from his clothes.
- *Eleventh Station*: He is nailed to the cross.
- *Twelfth Station*: Jesus dies on the cross on top of hill of Golgotha/ Calvary.
- *Thirteenth Station*: His body is taken down from the cross.
- *Fourteenth Station*: Jesus is buried in the Holy Sepulchre - the tomb which belonged to Joseph of Arimathea and given to Jesus.

* Stations 10-14 are inside the Church of the Holy Sepulchre.

The walk takes anywhere between 15 to 45 minutes depending on the pace of the group and the crowdedness of the Old City.

Note: Precautions mentioned in section under "Old City" apply especially to the Via Dolorosa.

One Friday in Jerusalem

Andre wrote another book about the Via Dolorosa. Growing up near *station eight*, he has a lot of insights from a local perspective. If you are interested to read it, the book is called "One Friday in Jerusalem" and the link for it can be found in the last page of this book.

Check out the **Introduction**:

The Via Dolorosa—Latin for "Way of Grief," "Way of Sorrows," or "Painful Way"—is a street in the Old City of Jerusalem, held to be the route that Jesus walked on the way to his crucifixion. It is a distance of about six hundred meters (two thousand feet) but a one-hour walk with prayers and devotions.

I know the Via Dolorosa because I grew up on the Via Dolorosa. As a boy, I played on its winding pathway, and for many years I have guided pilgrims retracing the footsteps of Jesus from Pilate's praetorium to Calvary. I know every doorway, every window overhead, every arch and column, the color, texture, and peculiarities of its walls. If every stone in the pavement had a name, I could call out each one individually. The interiors of sites such as the Church of the Holy Sepulchre are as familiar to me as your living room is to you.

But this book is so much more than a guided tour of the Via Dolorosa. It is certainly that—it will steer you from one site to the next down the narrow, stony pathway. But it is also a guide to greater depth in your relationship with Jesus, to the wonders of God's Word, to lives lived in the shadow of persecution and the power of the cross, and to your own life. In taking you faithfully through the stations of the cross, it will also transport you far beyond them on an eye-opening journey through the Bible, set against the background of Middle Eastern culture, customs, and history.

Very importantly, I hope this book will help you personalize, to the extent such a thing is possible, what Jesus endured as He bore His cross along the "Way of Sorrow." I want these pages to awaken your imagination, your emotions, and your heart so you will feel something of what Jesus might have felt and seen and thought, and so appreciate all the more the price He paid for you and me on that tragic, glorious day of His crucifixion. I hope this will be your experience as you read.

By the request of the many groups I have guided, this book will also share my personal story as a Palestinian Maronite Arab Christian. Growing up here in the roily tension zone of three great world religions—Christianity, Judaism, and Islam—I connect intimately with each one of the stations of the cross. As I share with you key passages of my life, I hope you will see in some of them reflections of your own life—for we all, each one of us, are bearing crosses of different sizes, shapes, and weights down our own Via Dolorosas. And the Spirit of Jesus is carrying us along beyond our griefs toward a glory greater than we can imagine.

Finally, I hope this book will awaken you to the plight of your brothers and sisters here in Jerusalem and in the Middle East. I desire that you will feel moved . . .

by compassion, as you hear the stories of these dark streets and darker lives;

by wonder, as you learn how God is actively changing men and women—Jews, Muslims, and Christians alike—in miraculous ways through the light of the gospel, the love of Jesus, and the power of the Holy Spirit;

to action, as you discover how you can come alongside your brothers and sisters here in the Middle East—and why it is so important, for both our sake and your own, that you do so.

CHAPTER NINETEEN

Holy Sepulchre Church

The Church of the Holy Sepulchre is built on the traditionally recognized site of Jesus' crucifixion, burial, and resurrection.

When compared to the ornate and lavish St Peter's Church in Rome, the humble Holy Sepulchre Church is not what tourists usually expect as they enter into the holiest Christian site in the world. Upon first contact with the church, one may be surprised by its less than striking exterior, but inside, the church is a fascinating conglomerate of 30-plus ornate chapels and worship spaces.

Background

The Church of the Holy Sepulchre was first built by Emperor Constantine the Great in the mid 320s after excavations showed evidence that supports the events of the Gospels – namely the True Cross and the Tomb.

It then enjoyed around 600 years of protection under different empires, including Muslim and Moorish rulers, until it was destroyed in the 11th century. The church was then rebuilt by the Crusaders and changed hands several times again. The structure standing today is more or less from the Crusader period (with additions) and smaller than the original.

Status Quo

The church today is run by six different denominations – Roman Catholic, Greek Orthodox, Syriac Orthodox, Armenians, Coptics, and Ethiopians.

Rivalry and violence over the years led to the Status Quo Agreement in 1856, which prevents any major changes or renovations unless unanimously agreed upon. The church more or less remained the same since then.

To avoid further clashes, the keys to the church have been in the hands of two Muslim families (Nusseibeh and Judeh) for centuries, and they alone have the privilege of locking and unlocking the gate daily.

Accessibility

The entrance to the church is free of charge and open to anyone from any background or religion. That being said, it is one of the most crowded sites in Israel. The only restriction upon entering the church is the strict modest dress code. Make sure your tourists are properly dressed for entering a holy site, meaning shoulders and knees covered. The church visit usually lasts between 1-2 hours, and there is no seating inside, so comfortable footwear is advisable.

Please note that visiting the Holy Sepulchre requires flexibility as large numbers of people or processions and mass(communion) may limit our access to and within the church.

Bathrooms

Bathrooms are available but strongly not recommended as they are not regularly cleaned nor maintained. It is best to carry tissues or toilet paper as they Old City bathrooms run out of toilet paper and do not often get replaced.

Navigating the Church

Navigating the church's chapels without a guide is a bit of a challenge, and therefore make sure to stay in one group and that no one strays far behind. There is only one gate to the church, which serves as both its entrance and exit. In the rare incident that one gets lost amongst the crowds, they can easily find their way back to the courtyard right outside the gate and wait for the group to come back around.

The first site inside the church is up a steep and narrow flight of steps to Calvary/Golgotha. There you will find the traditional place of the crucifixion and death of Christ. A queue of people can be seen waiting to touch the tip of the hill, located under the altar. If any wish to wait in line, communicate with the guide as the lines may take time.

Be aware that the steps up may be difficult for some, depending on the individuals of the group. If so, the individuals can wait for the group to come back down and continue the tour together.

Once back down, the guide will proceed to lead the group through the different chapels commemorating different events related to the crucifixion, ending at the Rotunda, which hosts the Tomb of Jesus – the Holy "Sepulchre." Please keep in mind that the top of the cave has long been carved out to allow more visitors, so what you will see is the edicule over the bedrock where the tomb was.

Standing in line to enter the tomb and touch the stone can take anywhere between twenty minutes and three hours, so depending on time, schedule, and desire of the group, you may or may not visit the tomb from the inside. If the group does indeed visit the tomb, please limit the person to three minutes maximum to allow more people to enter.

Location and Alternative Option

The location of the Church of the Holy Sepulchre inside the Old City may be a bit confusing at first as the scriptures say that Jesus was crucified and buried outside the city. However, the walls of the Old City today are not the same walls of the 1st Century. This area was, in fact, outside the walls during the time of the crucifixion. Nevertheless, since the 19th century, an alternative option for Golgotha was discovered right outside Damascus Gate [more in the next chapter].

CHAPTER TWENTY

The Garden Tomb

Unearthed in the mid-19th century, the Garden Tomb serves as an alternative site for the resurrection of Jesus. The Garden Tomb, as its name suggests, is a peaceful garden with a rock-cut tomb – perfectly resembling the setting of the story in the Gospels. Both the Holy Sepulchre and the Garden Tomb are usually included in the itinerary.

The Garden Tomb visit includes a tour around the beautiful garden, a lookout to the Skull Hill nearby (Golgotha), a visit inside the tomb itself (Spoiler alert: it's empty!), and a lovely private time for the group to worship together and share communion.

The entrance to the Garden Tomb is free of charge. However, an area for worship and sharing communion requires pre-booking and includes a small fee.

The communion elements are provided by the Garden Tomb (Twins Tours additionally provides complimentary wine cups made of olive wood, which may be kept as souvenirs). Amongst the communion supplies is an offering basket for those who would like to contribute to the Garden Tomb to help maintain this beautiful site. The Tour Leader is kindly required to return the communion supplies and basket to the main desk at the end of the stay.

After a bathroom break, the group may proceed to the gift shop through which is the exit. The group will assemble right outside the gift shop and, once everyone is counted, will continue to the bus together. Make sure no one tries making their way back to the bus alone as it may not be there.

CHAPTER TWENTY ONE

The City of David

The City of David is one of the more logistically complicated sites you will visit on your trip to Israel. It is a little more challenging physically (steep descents, stairs, and tunnels), which makes it likely that some people either will not be physically able to cope with the area or will choose to only participate in some of the sites on offer. This means, you have to ensure that all participants have a clear understanding of the potential challenges of the site, the timing and various meeting points. It is best to take care of this before arriving at the site to speed up the ticketing process.

Upon arrival, the tour guide will check in at the ticket office, which is located at the entrance to the Visitors Center. Given the popularity of the site, this can take some time.

They will also hand over the voucher and the confirmation form (provided in advance by the Twins Tours) and tell the ticket office how many people will participate in each section of the tour. A separate ticket is given for each of the following sections:

- 3D movie.
- Warren's Shaft.
- Davidson Center (this may not apply to your group).

If your tour guide is not provided by Twins Tours and is an external foundation tour guide provided by the City of David, he/she will meet you at the Visitors Center (the cashier at the ticket office will guide where to find your group).

Hand over your tickets to the guide as soon as you meet up with them. At this point, you should also tell the guide if any of the group will be leaving the tour before the end due to health problems / physical limitations.

There are several seating areas for groups around the Visitors Center complex, so while you are taking care of the tickets, advise your group to use the toilet and to fill their water bottles before meeting back at the designated seating area. It is very important that people do not leave their bags unattended in the Visitors Center.

At this point, any participants who have forgotten to bring water with them can purchase a bottle at the coffee shop. Those who need to buy flashlights or water shoes can do so at the Gift Shop adjacent to the Visitors Center (for speed and convenience, it would be better if people bring both of these items with them). Both the coffee shop and the gift shop accept credit cards, and there is an ATM machine next to the shop.

If participants purchase items in the gift shop, the cashier will ask for the name of their tour guide or name of the tour agency. If the purchase exceeds $118 USD (or the equivalent in other currency), tour participants should ask for a VAT form with the receipt, which can be redeemed at the airport for a VAT refund. (The tour guide/tour agent will be happy to assist with this process at the airport).

Movie Theater/Observation Deck

The guide will decide whether to start the tour on the observation deck or at the 3D movie (15 minutes). The 3D-movie appointment time is not flexible! You must be there exactly at the time printed on your ticket or you will not be allowed in.

The movie theater is located up a flight of 25 stairs (outside in sunshine /rain). The Observation Deck (15-20 minutes) is located up a further flight of uncovered stairs.

In general, there is not much shade, so remind people to bring a hat and sunglasses, and keep reminding them to drink.

Because there may be other groups entering the movie theater at the same time, find your seats quickly and try to sit together as a group. Tell anyone who wears prescription lenses to put the 3D-plastic glasses over their glasses.

Once the group descends from the movie/observation deck, allow another quick toilet/water break. Make sure that people know this is the last opportunity to use the facilities for at least 30 minutes (there are toilets at the end of the tour near the Pool of Siloam).

If there are people who cannot go down the stairs necessary to enter the archaeology sections, seat them in the Visitors Center and create an alternate plan for them.

Important: Make sure that anyone who is going any further than the 3D-Movie or observation deck is wearing shoes with good grips, such as sneakers or even walking boots.

David's Palace

Once the rest of the group is together, descend 15 metal steps to the David's Palace (15 minutes) archeology section which is situated directly underneath the Visitors Center. Ensure that the group stays close to the guide to allow other groups to pass by and to ensure that no one strays off with the wrong group.

If people are able to handle 15 stairs each way, they can join for just this portion, and return to the Visitors Center once the guide finishes the explanation for this section.

The Royal Quarter

Access to the next section, The Royal Quarter – "Area G" is down 55 fairly steep metal steps and 25 stone steps (80 steps in total, with a handrail). Do not allow people to do this section if they have problems with knees, or hips, or they are very tired.

The guide will speak for 15-20 minutes here. While there are a couple of possible places for groups to sit, the number of groups passing through means that seating is not always readily available.

Warren's Shaft

The descent into Warren's Shaft is steep and can be slippery at times. Do not let anyone attempt to enter in flip-flops or sandals. It is not possible to visit Warren's Shaft and then exit the site. The exit is via either the wet/dry tunnels.

Those people who chose not to go into Warren's Shaft and then onwards to the tunnels can return to the gift shop area to meet up with other members of the group.

This is a very popular site, and many groups will want to enter. Ensure you keep everyone together and do not block other groups from getting ahead of you.

The Wet/Dry Tunnels

Before you enter the wet/dry tunnels, please explain to the group that they can choose whichever route they prefer. They both lead to the

Pool of Siloam, either directly (the wet tunnel) or indirectly (the dry tunnel/Canaanite Tunnel).

The wet tunnel is 500m long, with chilled water that can reach up to 70cm/ 28 inches.

Encourage those planning on walking through the wet tunnel to hand over any valuables, such as cameras, phones, wallets, etc. that might get wet to fellow group members who are going through the dry tunnel.

People going into the wet tunnel need time to change their shoes and roll up trousers etc. Note: people cannot go in barefoot if they do not have water shoes; they have to continue through the dry tunnel.

Ensure that people who want to go in the wet tunnel bring suitable water shoes and a change of clothing with them

Both the wet/dry tunnels are quite low and narrow, making them unsuitable for those who are taller/bigger than average. Please be sensitive when discussing this with your group.

Make sure that people understand that the only way out of the wet/dry tunnels is to go all the way through them. Once inside, there is no way to turn back, so if anyone knows they are claustrophobic or is worried about being in a confined, dark space, it's probably best that they do not go inside at all.

For safety/security, ask people to volunteer to be the first into the tunnel and, more importantly, to bring up the rear to make sure everyone gets in and out safely. If people forget their flashlights, make sure to distribute them among the group to make the way as visible as possible. Tell people to take it slowly, especially the person at the front. Make sure to communicate down the line if a particularly low or narrow spot is coming up so people can feel prepared and to prevent any sore heads!

The Siloam Pool

You can arrange for those people who did not go through Warren's Shaft/Tunnels to meet you by the Pool of Siloam via an alternate route. The ascent back to the visitor's center is very steep and can be quite challenging. We recommend that everyone uses the shuttles provided by the site for speed and convenience. They cost 5 nis a person, and the price is not included in the ticket, so please make sure to have petty cash to cover this charge.

Important: Make sure to tell the group that the water in the pool is not drinkable.

Learnings/Readings

- Biblical references to the City of David are found in the book of Lamentations, the book of Jeremiah chapters 34-38.
- Nehemiah begins to rebuild city walls here.
- According to the Gospel of John, Jesus healed the blind man at the Siloam Pool (John 9:1-11).
- When the temple stood in Jerusalem, a ceremony called Nisuch ha-Mayim (lit. "Pouring of the water") or Water Libation Ceremony was performed every morning during the Sukkot holiday (Tabernacles). The water for the ceremony was drawn up from the Pool of Siloam. Today it is remembered in the celebration of Simchat Beit Ha'Shoeva (Rejoicing at the Place of the Water-Drawing) during Sukkot.

CHAPTER TWENTY TWO

The Temple Mount

The Temple Mount, known in Arabic as Haram al Sharif (the Noble Sanctuary), is one of the most hotly contested religious sites in the world. Sacred to Jews and Christians and Muslims, the site is currently an Islamic holy site, tightly controlled by the Jordanian government through the Waqf administration.

Important: The rules for non-Muslims visiting the Temple Mount and tourist conduct at the site are very strict. It is forbidden to mention anything about the Jewish Temple while at the site, or even after you have exited the Temple Mount and entered the Muslim Quarter. There will be people (self-appointed guards) closely following your group and monitoring what is said and what questions are asked.

Should anything even slightly controversial or inflammatory be mentioned – even if it seems harmless and is completely innocent – it could inflame anger (including violence) towards the group. At best, there could be angry shouting; at worst, it could lead to a violent mob that necessitates a police escort to ensure your group leaves the area safely.

Make sure to brief your group in advance so they can understand how the temple mount site is extreemley sensitive.

To avoid any possible interference with your group, like locals shouting or cursing at you, it is best to let the local guide handle all the explanations. They know what can and can't be said and will not make an innocent mistake that could have serious repercussions. Your local guide knows where to stop and where not to go, so follow him as a group – this is not the place you want to wander on your own.

Access to the Temple Mount

In theory, non-Muslims can go up to the Temple Mount from Sunday-Thursday. Given the sensitive nature of the Temple Mount, however, there is no guarantee that the site will be open to visitors when you intend to visit. Access is decided on a day-by-day and sometimes even minute-by-minute basis by the Israeli police and operates according to the current security situation.

Even when things are calm and non-Muslims allowed to go up to the Temple Mount, there are stringent opening and closing times for visitors. This is to ensure only Muslims are on the Haram al Sharif during the five daily prayer times.

The best way to maximize your chance of getting onto the Temple Mount is to be at the checkpoint, which is located next to the Western Wall, at 7.00 am so as not to get stuck behind other groups and wasting a lot of time in queuing.

If you are visiting in the summer, make sure to bring plenty of sunscreen and water and make sure everyone is wearing a hat as the Temple Mount is very exposed with limited shade.

Visiting the Temple Mount

Entry to the Temple Mount for non-Muslims is through the Mughrabi (Moroccan) Gate – entrance to the wooden walkway and security is located close to the Dung Gate and Western Wall. To go up to the Temple Mount, you must go through tight security and may be asked to show your passport.

To speed up the process, it's best not to carry any backpacks and certainly not to carry anything that can be seen as a weapon (either offensive or defensive). Visitors cannot enter the site with any sacred or religious objects, such as bibles. Nor can they take iPads, professional cameras (cameras with large lenses), pictures, or musical instruments. And they should certainly not enter with alcohol, which is forbidden in Islam. Any "offending" objects will be confiscated by security at the entrance to the site.

Brief the group in advance to make sure everyone is dressed modestly. Neither men nor women should wear shorts or tight jeans. Women are advised to cover up as much as possible, even wearing a scarf around their neck. A headscarf is not required.

Remind the group to remove any religious paraphernalia, such as crosses or any other Jewish and Christian symbols. It is best to leave these somewhere safe and not to carry them on your person.

Behavior on the Temple Mount

Make sure the group understands there are very strict rules of behavior on the Temple Mount.

The group should be reminded to behave with extreme modesty. Any touching between men and women (even husband and wife) is forbidden. Forbidden touching ranges from kissing to holding hands. Stress that separation is necessary, even while taking pictures.

155

Make sure that no one prays or sings at the site, or even gives the impression of praying as this is absolutely forbidden and will put the group in potential danger. This rule is also true for Jewish groups and is part of the "status quo" that governs religious life and behavior in Jerusalem.

The Dome of the Rock, the Al Aqsa Mosque and the other mosques on the Temple Mount are strictly forbidden to non-Muslims. Make sure no one tries to enter them or even tries to take photos of the interiors, even with a long-distance zoom lens.

Remind the group not to try to take any "souvenirs" from the site. Taking any dirt, stones, or even any kind of trees or branches from the Temple Mount complex is strictly forbidden.

Remember, you might not agree with the rules, but they have to be followed. Save any discussion about it until you are safely back on the bus or at the hotel. Even when you exit the Temple Mount into the Muslim Quarter, do not say or do anything that could possibly offend the local population.

Bathrooms

There are bathrooms on the Temple Mount. However, they are squat toilets and not western style. To avoid any discomfort or confusion, make sure to have a bathroom break before ascending to the Temple Mount or wait for the next stop to go to the toilets as it is not advisable to split from the group on your own.

CHAPTER TWENTY THREE

The Western Wall

Background

The Western Wall is one of the holiest sites in Jewish tradition and is the holiest site at which Jews are permitted to pray. Only the Temple Mount, upon which Jewish prayer is forbidden, is more holy.

The Wall is a small section of a retaining wall erected as part of the expansion of the Second Temple during Herod's rule.

In Hebrew, the Western Wall is known as the Kotel. It is also known – although not by Jews – as the Wailing Wall, as it is the place where Jews have wept over the destruction of the Second Temple and also a place of intense and meaningful prayer.

What to Wear

Modest clothing is important for men and women when visiting the Old City of Jerusalem and especially when visiting the Western Wall. To make sure no one in the group is embarrassed or risks offending anyone, check before you leave the hotel that everyone has the correct clothing. This will make it much more pleasant for everyone and is also a sign of respect for those who will be praying at this holy site.

- **Women** should make sure their elbows and upper legs are covered. If they have bare arms or legs, they should put on a shawl over the shoulders and tie a shawl around their waste to make a skirt. If they have forgotten to bring a cover-up, there are shawls that can be borrowed at the entrance to the wall (Prayer Area) and women "guards" who make sure everyone is dressed correctly.

- **Men** should make sure their heads are covered (this is true for any Jewish religious site). There are skull caps available to borrow at the entrance to the men's side of the wall. They should also make sure not to have bare arms (no vest tops) or very short shorts.

Entering the Western Wall Area

For security reasons, everyone must pass through a metal detector and have their bags searched before entering the Western Wall Plaza area. To speed up the process, make sure you aren't carrying any glass items or weapons, such as pocket knives.

At the Western Wall Plaza

Once you pass through security, you will enter the Western Wall Plaza.

If you visit on a Monday or Thursday morning, the Plaza and the prayer area are likely to be very busy. On these two days, the Torah (the five books of Moses) is read during the morning service. It is also a day that 13-year-old boys celebrate their bar mitzvahs, so you are likely to see groups of people being led by drummers or other musicians as the young boys are feted and celebrated as they read from the Torah for the very first time.

Western Wall Visit Do's and Don'ts

- The Wall is an important site in Judaism, but it is open for everyone to come and visit and say a prayer or to sit with God in their own way. Don't be afraid or embarrassed to go right up to the Wall and to touch and feel it and to connect with its history.

- When it comes to proper behavior, just think about what is respectful and polite. You will see a lot of groups of children, teenagers, and even soldiers – and they will not be quiet! There will be shouting and singing and displays of noise, especially in the Plaza. At the Wall, you should be quieter and more mindful of those around you who are praying and having a personal moment with God. Do not disturb them with loud talking or laughing.

- One of the traditions associated with the Wall is to leave a note in the cracks in the wall (you'll notice little pieces of paper crammed into the cracks of the wall as you approach it). If you want, add your prayer to the hundreds of thousands of others. You can write a personal prayer or plea, a request, or a dream. It is common for people to make a prayer for a sick relative or friend, asking for divine help in their cure. You can write whatever you want and know that no one is ever going to read it. The Wall is cleared of notes twice a year. The notes themselves are considered to be holy and like other holy Jewish texts are buried in consecrated ground on the Mount of Olives.

- If the prayer area is especially crowded, you may find it hard to get up to the Wall. Be polite and ask people to move for you. There are certain prayers during which people cannot move, so if you see someone praying very intently, wait until they are finished before asking them to move out of your way.

- You can take pictures, including selfies, at the Wall, however, be respectful of others and try to avoid taking photos of other people, unless you ask their permission.

- Do not take a photo from the men's section into the women's section (and vice versa). People can get very angry if they think the proper laws of separation/modesty are not being adhered to. If you want to take a photo of people praying, it's best to do it from the Plaza.

- You can use your phone, but it's necessary to exit the prayer area and head back to the Plaza to talk.

- If you want to use social media apps or a live video, do it from the Plaza rather than up close to the wall.

- You will notice many people walking backwards away from the Wall. This is because, like you would not turn your back on a king or member of royalty, you shouldn't turn your back on God. Some people will walk backwards the entire way, others will take a few symbolic steps backwards and then walk out of the prayer area in the regular way.

- Do not hand out any religious material at the Wall or the Plaza. This could land you in serious trouble. There are special religious police at the Wall, as well as a lot of security.

- If someone comes up to you and tries to give you religious material or talk about the Moshiach (the Hebrew name for the Messiah), do not explain why you believe Jesus is the Messiah. It's best not to engage these people in conversation and to politely hand back any materials they may try to give you.

- It is common for people to ask you for charity at the Wall. It is up to you if you want to give them any money, but it is not expected.

Information for Visiting on the Jewish Sabbath

Visiting the Western Wall on the Jewish Sabbath (from Friday night to Saturday night) carries a few extra restrictions not in place during the rest of the week, but it also carries an extra special flavor as Jews celebrate the holiest and most special day of their week.

If you are at the Wall on a Friday evening/night at around sundown, the wall will be incredibly busy with groups celebrating the start of the Sabbath with a special prayer service. There is likely to be alot of noise, singing, and dancing.

Owing to strictures against using electricity on the Sabbath, taking photographs is forbidden, so you will have to store the memories in your head rather than digitally. Be respectful of others' observance of the Sabbath, and don't try to sneak photographs. Not only is this disrespectful, but people take any violation very seriously and will get annoyed with anyone they see breaking the rules, which can be upsetting and embarrassing for everyone concerned.

Making the Most of Your Time at the Western Wall

Visiting the Western Wall can be a very intense and overwhelming experience. There is a lot of noise, people, and very limited shade. It's easy for people to get lost or confused.

Set a meeting spot for the group to reassemble once they have visited the Wall. Set a fixed time for everyone to meet back again – you don't want to have to go chasing after stragglers in this open, busy area.

The tour guide will not go down to the Wall; he will wait at a designated spot in the Plaza.

Point out to the group that there are bathrooms for them to use to the left of the Plaza. They can also fill up water bottles here.

Point out the big water fountain in the plaza with the double-handed pitchers. Explain that these are for ritual hand washing and are not to be used for drinking water.

Common Questions

1. *What exactly are people doing at the Western Wall?*
    Many people are praying close to the Wall and in the prayer areas. Others will be sitting in silent contemplation, others sitting and talking quietly. This is a holy site and the place where people come to pray, cry, and plead with God.

2. *Why is the Western Wall sometimes called the "Wailing Wall"?*
    According to the Talmud (the central text of Judaism), when the Second Temple was destroyed, all the Gates of Heaven were closed, except for one, which was known as the "Gate of Tears." Throughout the centuries, Jews have come to cry out to God to rebuild Jerusalem. This tearful (wailing) prayer gave the wall one of its most common names.

3. *Why are men and women separated?*
    In Orthodox Judaism, men and women always sit separately during prayer.

4. *Why is the men's section so much bigger than the women's section?*
    Men are required to pray three times a day while there is no such demand placed on women, so more men tend to visit than women. Also, men have to pray as part of a minyan, a quorum of 10 men, whereas women pray individually.

5. *I notice people rocking back and forth, or bending over, what are they doing?*
    The rocking back and forth is common during prayer. It's not a religious rule, but it is something that a lot of people seem to do.

The bending over happens during a specific prayer when God's name is mentioned. It's a sign of respect – like bowing before a king.

6. *What are the books lying around?*
These are prayer books containing the three daily prayer services, as well as various other prayers and services. There are also Bibles, books of Psalms, and other types of prayer books. You can look through them and see if they have a translation in English. If you do pick a book up, be careful not to drop it on the floor and treat it with respect. If you accidentally drop it, it is custom to pick it up straight away and to kiss the cover (you don't have to kiss the book, but please pick it up and put back where it was).

7. *Can I sit in the chairs/move them around?*
Of course, they are for everyone.

8. *Why are some men covering their heads with what looks like a blanket?*
These "blankets" are prayer shawls that all married men wear when praying. They cover their heads to help them concentrate on their prayer and to block out some of the noise and the distraction going on around them.

9. *Why are some men wearing furry "cheese wheel" hats?*
These large, furry hats are called shtreimels (a Yiddish word) and are worn by married men who belong to one of the ultra-Orthodox Hasidic sects. Members of these sects are called Hasidim, and they wear these hats on the Sabbath, Jewish holidays, or other festive occasions. If the hats look like a throwback to 18th century Poland, that's because they are. Hasidim follow a strict dress code that has its origins in the beginnings of the Hasidic movement, which started in Poland in the 18th century.

10. What is the red string that people are giving out?

Some people believe that the red strings ward off the evil eye and are a good luck symbol. The belief is rooted in Jewish folk law and has gained some prominence since Madonna made Kabbalah popular. If the idea speaks to you, go ahead and get one! You will have to make a small monetary donation, and the belief is you should wear it until it falls off.

11. I see teenagers who are not dressed as soldiers carrying guns. Should I be worried?

Guns are a fact of life in Israel where the majority of teenagers, male and female, serve in the army for two-three years. You will often see people not dressed in uniform toting guns. These teens might be in the army but on leave. They are not required to wear a uniform, but according to law, they cannot leave their guns unattended. While there are many guns visible in the streets, incidents of shootings are incredibly low.

Western Wall Tunnel Tours

Location

The entrance into the tunnels is on the northern side of the Western Wall plaza, a few meters away from the Western Wall. Upon entering, visitors walk through a series of rooms moving eastward until they hit the Western Wall. From that point on the tunnels continue straight northward directly along the Western Wall until the west-northern most point. During their walk in the tunnels, visitors will pass by Second Temple era homes, ancient cisterns, constructions from the Muslim period, an aqueduct from the Hasmonean period and more.

Visiting the Western Wall Tunnels requires pre-booking as it is a very popular site with limited empty spots for groups. Twins Tours will book the tour for your group at least three months in advance.

During the guided tour inside this tunnel you will learn about and see the fascinating story of ancient Jerusalem and how it continues to be meticulously discovered underground, dug out slowly and carefully. You will see stones, models and actual structures which provide clues as to how the Second Temple was constructed. In addition, these artifacts help explain the history of this area through the eyes of all the great empires that once ruled Jerusalem.

The tunnels run along approximately 488 meters of the Western Wall, giving visitors a taste for the challenge that stood before Herod the Great during this biggest of all his immense building projects—the expansion of the Temple Mount. One such example is the famous western stone which is 14 meters long and weighs almost 570 tons.

The tour lasts around 75 minutes.

History

These complex underground tunnels create a direct link between the history of the Hasmonean period and modern times. The tunnels are supported by many arches and contain stairways that connected the ancient city with the Temple Mount, over the Tyropoeon Valley that ran along the western side of the Temple Mount, separating the two. Today these passageways support streets and homes in the Muslim Quarter.

The tunnels were first discovered during digs done by British archaeologists in the 19th century, but the real digging was done after the Six Day War, after 1967, by the Israeli Ministry of Religions. One of the most special places to visit inside the tunnels is the part of the Western Wall traditionally considered closest to where the Holy of Holies used to be on the Temple Mount. The Holy of Holies, where the Foundation Stone and the Dome of the Rock are located, is the holiest place for Jews. In this location in the tunnels, there is a small synagogue where Jews come to pray.

CHAPTER TWENTY FOUR

What to See on Your Free Day

(Please check with your guide first as you may have visited some of these sites already. Please call ahead to verify hours and fees as there may be group discounts).

Rockefeller Archeological Museum

Sultan Suleiman St 27, Jerusalem

This museum houses a large number of artifacts from excavations taking place during the British Mandate.

(Sunday, Monday, Wednesday and Thursday 10:00 to 15:00; Saturday and Holidays 10:00 to 14:00; closed Tuesday and Friday)

No Entrance Fee

Tel: 02-6282251

The Burnt House

2 Tiferet Israel St, Jerusalem

Visit the magnificent remains of a burnt house from the time of the destruction of the Second Temple and the upper part of Jerusalem.

(Opens Sunday to Thursday 9:00-19:00, Friday 9:00-1:00, closed on Saturday)

Entrance Fee: Adult 25 ILS

Tel: 02-6287211

Yad Vashem Memorial Museum

Har Hazikaron (Mt. Remembrance)

Visit the beautiful yet tragic memorial for the Holocaust victims.

(Open Monday, Tuesday, Wednesday 8:30-17:00, Thursday 8:30-20:00, Friday 8:30-14:00, closed on Saturday and Sunday)

No Entrance Fee

Tel: 02-6443400

Yemin Moshe Neighborhood and Montefiore's Windmill

Stroll through the picture-perfect neighborhood which was established due to the overcrowding within the Old City itself.

The Israel Museum

Derech Ruppin 11, Jerusalem

Check out the wonderful exhibits and the Shrine of the Book (Dead Sea Scrolls).

Christ Church Coffee Shop

Jaffa Gate across the Tower of David Museum.

(Open daily 9:00-20:00, Sundays 9:00-16:00)

Tel: 02-6277727

Jerusalem Biblical Zoo & Aquarium

Derech Aharon Shulov 1

Stroll through the beautiful park with over 170 diverse species of Biblical and endangered animals.

(Open everyday: Sunday through Thursday 9:00-19:00, Friday 9:00-16:30, Saturday 10:00-18:00)

Entrance Fee: Adult/Child 40 ILS

Tel: 02-6750111

(Open Daily: Sunday, Monday, Wednesday, Thursday 10:00-17:00, Tuesday 16:00-21:00, Friday 10:00-14:00, Saturday 10:30-16:00)

Entrance Fee: Adult 54 ILS

Tel: 02-6708888

City of David

Ma'alot Ir David St, Jerusalem

Visit the place where it all began! Journey back to the time when King David conquered and made Jerusalem his capital and enjoy the walk through Hezekiah's tunnel.

(Open Sunday to Friday 8:00-17:00, closed on Saturday)

Entrance Fee: Adult 65 ILS

Tel: 02-6268700

Temple Institute

Misgav Ladach St 40, Jerusalem

See and understand the story of the Holy Temple

(Sunday to Thursday 9:00-17:00, Friday 9:00-14:00. Closed on Saturday)

Entrance Fee: Adult 25 ILS, Guide, additional 70 ILS. (Group discounts available)

Tel: 02-6264545

Haas Promenade

Daniel Yanofsky Street

Enjoy a spectacular panoramic view of Jerusalem!

Tower of David Museum

Jaffa Gate 9114001, Jerusalem

This museum tells the story of the 4000-year-old Jerusalem. Be sure to look out for the incredible Night Show events!

(Open Daily: 9:00-16:00/17:00, Saturday 9:00-14:00)

Entrance Fee: Adult 40 ILS

Tel: 02-6265333

Bible Lands Museum

Shmuel Stephan Weiz St 21

Explore the different cultures of the ancient peoples of the Bible.

(Open Monday, Tuesday, Thursday 9:30-17:30, Wednesday 9:30-21:30, Friday 10:00-14:00, closed on Sunday and Saturday)

Entrance Fee: Adult 44 ILS

Tel: 02-5611066

169

Alliance Church

Al Rusul St 14, Old City of Jerusalem

Worship with the local Arab believers in the heart of Old City Jerusalem.

(Service: Sunday 10:30)

Tel: 02-6260711

King of Kings

Jaffa St 97

Visit the English Messianic Congregation in the city center of Jerusalem.

(Service: Sunday 17:00)

Tel: 02-6251899

Christ Church

Jaffa Gate

The oldest Protestant Church in the Middle East, instrumental in the return of the Jewish people to Israel.

(Services: Sunday 9:30 and 19:00)

Tel: 02-6277727

Nazarene Church in Nazareth

Paulus VI St, Nazareth

Worship with the local Arab Christians in Nazareth.

(Service: Friday 18:30, Sunday 10:00)

Tel: 04-6553062

St. Andrew's Tiberias, the Church of Scotland

Gdud Barak St 1, Tiberias

Visit the ecumenical English-speaking church in the heart of the ancient city of Tiberias by the Sea of Galilee.

(Service: Sunday 10:00)

Tel: 054-2446736

V. When You Return

- When you return home, you will feel excited to share with your church, school, and community your experience and what God has done in your life during your visit to Israel.

- You may want to plan an 'Israel Night' and invite friends or family and share your experiences through stories, pictures, or videos you took. Some people even serve simple Israeli food to make the night complete!

- Twins Tours is always happy to receive individual and group feedback once you are back home and have time to reflect on your Tour, and organize another one for next year.

Study Resources

Building a foundation will help orientate your group to the geographical, cultural, and historical context of the land of the Bible, and will help tour participants get the most out of their trip. Below are some resources we recommend that can either be studied as a group or individually:

- Film: The Jerusalem Film – an IMAX film by National Geographic
- DVD: That The World May Know: Faith Lessons – Ray Vander Laan
- The Israelis: Ordinary People in an Extraordinary Land – Dana Rosenfeld
- Book: Jesus Through Middle Eastern Eyes: Cultural Studies in the Gospels – Kenneth E. Bailey
- Book: Our Father Abraham: Jewish Roots of the Christian Faith – Marvin R. Wilson
- Book: The Source – James A. Michener
- Book: One Friday in Jerusalem – Andre Moubarak www.onefridayinjerusalem.com/shop
- Book: The Lemon Tree: An Arab, a Jew, and the Heart of the Middle East – Sandy Tolan
- Book: Blood Brothers: The Unforgettable Story of a Palestinian Christian Working for Peace in Israel – Elias Chacour
- Website: www.antiquities.org.il – Israel Antiquities Authority
- Website: www.akhlah.com/hebrew/worksheets/ – Jewish learning materials – try the alphabet lesson worksheets!
- Website: www.andremoubarak.com – To order all of Andre's books and invite him to speak and teach in your church.

What You Can Do

Whether you are an individual, a group, or a church, one simple and practical way you can help is this: Build a relationship with us.

All it takes is you. One person can make a huge difference—and we can make a difference for you. Make an effort to connect with us. Today's technology makes it possible. We will connect you with ministries and churches in the Middle East, especially in Israel, the West Bank, and Palestine.

In general, the churches in the West are tremendously blessed and yet so spoiled. We indigenous Christians are doing the hard work and still standing, persevering, and carrying our cross daily, even if it costs us our lives.

We are your link to reach the Middle East.

Please do not forget us or ignore us.

We invite you to come visit this land. You will be as safe as if you were walking the sidewalks of your hometown—perhaps even safer—as thousands of visitors from the West will tell you, and you will be in the best of hands. Let us share with you in person our narrative and heritage and help you discover the land in which our common faith is still rooted.

Jesus died and was resurrected to give us hope. Life for us Palestinian Christians often becomes very difficult here when there is open conflict, and many times I have thought of closing the Twins Tours office and moving away from Jerusalem permanently. However, I continue to hold on and hope for better days to come. I am always optimistic and looking for what Christ is doing even in the dark hours. I stay faithful and committed despite the obstacles constantly being thrown at us.

My heart and aim is that Christians in the West will become more aware of what is happening with their brothers and sisters in the East. I hope this book will inspire you to reach out to us, arrange for a group and meet your Middle Eastern families in Christ. And I hope you will respond to our invitation to experience the living faith of Jesus Christ here in the Holy Land.

Thanks, Thank you, Thank you for your assistance, Thank you for your consideration, Thank you for reading this book, Thank you for your time, Yours faithfully, Yours sincerely, Yours truly,

Andre Moubarak

About the Author

Andre Moubarak is co-owner of Twins Tours & Travel Ltd in Israel. He was born into an Arabic Catholic family along the Via Dolorosa, (The Way of the Cross), in the heart of the Christian quarter of Jerusalem. He encountered the living Jesus as his savior and that transformation sparked a revival in Jerusalem that continues to have an impact today.

His passion is teaching and leading others to encounter God through the Bible in Israel. He is an author and prayer warrior with a heart for revival, transformation and sanctification for all who travel to The Holy Land. He is joined with his wife, Marie, in a unique call and mission – to bring the reconciliation power of the gospel to all people in a land where people are divided.

Andre is an ordained gospel minister and a Licensed Tour Guide who leads numerous groups from around the world on tours of the Holy Land each year. He teaches about the Jewish roots of Jesus and the Kingdom of Heaven, prays for divine healing and guides the visiting groups of Christians through the land where God became flesh and dwelled among us. His unique teaching shines light on the scripture and how it applies to each biblical site. In addition, Andre personally ministers to each distinct group as he ignites the spirit through prayer and teaching. Each tour is a personal journey and invitation to link together the church from around the world into a network of praise as we prepare Jerusalem for the Messiah's return!

For more information, visit our website www.twinstours.org

More Exciting Books by the Author

One Friday in Jerusalem

A Road. A City. A Savior. And One Man's Story.

The Via Dolorosa. The "Way of Sorrow," held for centuries to be the road Jesus walked to His crucifixion. For countless believers across the world, it is the spiritual pilgrimage of a lifetime. For Andre Moubarak, it is his home and his life. Join Andre for a very special journey down this storied street he knows so intimately.

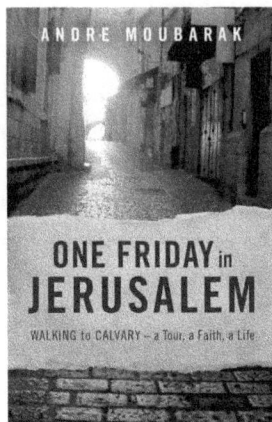

One Friday in Jerusalem puts you in the sandals of Jesus as He bore His cross the brutal half mile to Calvary. Contemplate the sweat, the smells, the swelling crowds, the bark of soldiers, and the agonizing realities of crucifixion. And hear why each station of the cross is so meaningful for Andre, a minority among minorities in an ethnically sundered land.

Providing unique Middle Eastern glimpses into the Bible, *One Friday in Jerusalem* is a tour book packed with historical, cultural, geographical, archaeological, and spiritual insights. It is a gripping reflection on the passion of Jesus. And it is the remarkable, true stories of a man who knows intimately the sorrows and struggle of the Via Dolorosa—and the joy, hope, and life-changing power of the risen Christ.

176

IN THE RIGHT HANDS THIS BOOK WILL CHANGE LIVES!

Most of the people, pastors, churches who like to visit Israel need this book, and Twins Tours & Travel Ltd is constantly seeking methods to spread the work of God all over the land.

Generosity Encouraged

Will you help us reach more people?

"Remember this: Whoever sows sparingly will also reap sparingly, and whoever sows generously will also reap generously." (2 Cor. 9:6).

EXTEND THIS MINISTRY BY SOWING

3 - Books

5 - Books

10 - Books

OR MORE TODAY

https://www.onefridayinjerusalem.com/shop

Study Reader Israel

This Study Guide reader is very usable whether you are traveling through Israel on your own or if you are part of a group guided tour. It is a great read to prepare before you come, or during your visit and even after your tour ends. It includes the geographical divisions of Israel, the feast of the Bible, updated facts about Israel. Almost every location in Israel is listed in alphabetical order with background information and biblical significance. This manual will give you additional information that you need to enrich your understanding of the Holy Land.

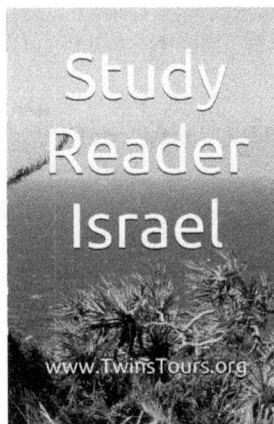

About the Founders

Andre & Tony Moubarak, the co-founders of Twins Tours, have a combined total of 25 years in the tourism industry. Andre and Tony are both licensed tour guides, operators and gifted Bible teachers. Twins Tours is dedicated to teaching the language, culture, and traditions of the biblical text to Christian pilgrims from all over the world.

One of our specialties is creating a tour where you see amazing Biblical sites and, at the same time, see what God is doing today through various ministries and organizations.

The fusion of these two elements creates an encounter that will extend your understanding beyond a traditional tour. This can range from a day or two of volunteer or service projects or as short of a time as a few hours of hearing from the 'living stones'.

Contact Us

Twins Tours & Travel LTD.
Jaffa Rd. 97, Clal Building
Floor C2, Office #201
P.O. Box 28314
Jerusalem 91283
Israel

Office Phone: +972 2-579-8159
Mobile: +972 54-523-1145
USA: +1(512) 222-3160
Fax: +972 2-579-8158
Skype: twinstours

E-mail: info@twinstours.com

Websites
http://www.twinstours.org
http://www.onefridayinjerusalem.com
htttp://www.andremoubarak.com

Follow us
Twitter: http://twitter.com/twinstours
Facebook: http://www.facebook.com/andre.moubarak
Instagram: http://instagram.com/twinstours

Subscribe to Andre's Podcast:
Walking the Land – https://apple.co/3bgZYxf

Become a Partner

Your generous donations help Twins Tours to keep going and moving forward. Your gifts help us to create content, write articles, produce audio and video teachings, online classes, study tours, and so much more.

Partner with us today and help our teachings reach more places around the world while witnessing your gifts multiply. Visit our website to see how you can help spread the word of God through your donations:

TwinsTours.org/ BecomeAPartner

Stay connected with Twins Tours via e-mail in order to receive our newsletters and stay updated with what the Lord is doing in the Holy Land.

Email: info@twinstours.com

Connect with Andre's personal number for videos and updates on WhatsApp: +972 54-523-1145

Blessings from Twins Tours

www.ingramcontent.com/pod-product-compliance
Lightning Source LLC
Chambersburg PA
CBHW031933090426
42811CB00002B/166